A PLACE FOR US GUYS

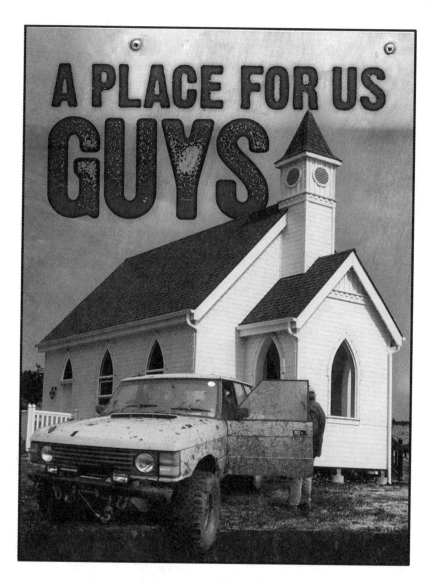

Charles Burkeen

Pacific Press® Publishing Association
Nampa, Idaho
Oshawa, Ontario, Canada
www.pacificpress.com

Copyright 2007 by
Pacific Press® Publishing Association
Printed in the United States of America
All rights reserved

Cover design by Mark Bond
Cover images: iStockphoto.com
Inside design by Steve Lanto

Library of Congress Cataloging-in-Publication Data

Burkeen, Charles, 1955-
A place for us guys / Charles Burkeen.
p. cm
ISBN 13: 978-0-8163-2193-3
ISBN 10: 0-8163-2193-0
1. Seventh-day Adventist men—Religious life. 2. Christian life—
Seventh-day Adventist authors. I. Title
BV4528.2.B875 2007
248.8'42—dc22
2006052728

You may obtain additional copies of this book by calling toll-free 1-800-
765-6955 or by visiting http://www.adventistbookcenter.com.

07 08 09 10 11 • 5 4 3 2 1

Dedicated to my mom, Betty Lou Dickerman.

This woman raised four guys

without losing her cool or her sanity.

Contents

There's a Guy Sitting in the Rain With a Laptop

It's an office only a guy could understand. The smell of musty canvas and the sound of grape-sized water pellets dripping from massive fir trees onto the roof bring comfort only to certain people. At least the heater still works, and the old canvas keeps out *most* of the rain.

I'm sitting in my twenty-something-year-old tent trailer parked alongside the picturesque ripples and waterfalls of Brice Creek, at the southern end of Oregon's Willamette Valley. This campground is little more than a wide spot in the road, the remnant of an old mining town now known simply as Hobo Camp. Every now and then, an explorer can find a rusty chunk of machinery jutting out of the bank, a crusty reminder that this was once a thriving gold-rush community. I'm currently the only hobo in Hobo Camp.

What is it that draws a guy like me, equipped with a Bible and a laptop, to a place called Hobo Camp? Is it the peace and solitude? Is it the rugged setting, miles from the nearest electric outlet? Is it the need to prove to myself that I can still survive as the miners did in days of old (though their cabins were certainly less watertight than my metal and canvas

9

cocoon)? Is it the fact that this primitive campground is still free and I am notoriously cheap? Well, that helps.

I've come in order to reflect on what it means to be a Seventh-day Adventist guy—as in simultaneously a Seventh-day Adventist and a guy. My question is, Are these two cultures truly compatible? Is it possible to be a definitely dedicated Seventh-day Adventist disciple of Christ and still maintain that integral part of your identity—being a guy—that makes you comfortable in your own skin?

What exactly is spirituality like for a guy—especially a Seventh-day Adventist Christian guy? I believe that the Bible gives insights into personal spirituality that even includes the sometimes gruff and often misunderstood world of guys.

So, what qualifies me to write on the spiritual issues that face Seventh-day Adventist guys? I don't have a master's degree in guyology. I'm not a psychologist, sociologist, anthropologist, or even an archaeologist. I can only draw on my personal experience as a guy.

I started young. I was a Cub Scout and then a Boy Scout. My mom is an honorary guy, since she was our den mother. She did all the little things to make our Cub Scout den a great haven of boyhood activities. And she cleaned up the mess after we were done each week.

I've been on a snipe hunt (I held the bag), and I have conducted snipe hunts without feeling a twinge of guilt. I played basketball in junior high, and I went out for track and cross-country in high school, where I earned the big letter C (for Cottage Grove High) that adorns the long-neglected school jacket in my closet. (It occasionally still fits.) I have worked in a lumber mill and on a fishing boat. I've been a plumber, a painter, and a general-construction handyman. I've been a gandy dancer (a railroad-track repairman) and a welder in a boxcar repair shop. In my previous life, I led a garage band named Redline—that line on your tachometer that warns you when your hot rod's engine is about to blow. (Our claim to fame was that we were the house band for a bar called the Suds Factory, and we were the favorite group of the local Free Souls motorcycle gang.)

I can shop for hours at G. I. Joes, "the Sports and Auto Store," but ten minutes in a shopping mall and my eyes glaze over, my ears begin ringing, and I'm looking for a sturdy bench to sit down on. I change the oil in our cars every three thousand miles, I do my own tune-ups, and last winter I replaced the transmission in my SUV all by myself. And I enjoy four-wheeling, especially with a winch on the front of the Jeep, a hi-lift jack, a shovel, and a chainsaw for those times when I drive farther than the road allows.

You've probably guessed by now that I haven't been a Seventh-day Adventist all my life. That came later and is another story. I have, however, been a Seventh-day Adventist pastor for nineteen years now, and a lot of my church members are guys. I've spoken to men's groups, which also include a lot of guys. I think I have the guy thing down!

I pray that this discussion will lead you into a deeper understanding of who you are in God's eyes. I hope you find this book to be a valuable tool for that exploration. I know that since guys are guys, group discussions are usually pretty short and often don't include any actual discussion, but I have included some personal reflection questions for you to consider, just between you and God. I assume that since you're reading this book, you do actually talk to God. If you don't, you should.

So, welcome to Hobo Camp. Join me as my beard grows, my neighborhood gathering of forest creatures grows (a skunk visited my camp on my first night), and our understanding of God's love for each of His children grows too.

CHAPTER 1

Why It's Normal to Be Crazy

It's October. Daylight hours are shrinking away as the sun heads south for the winter. The rains have come, and my lawn is golden with damp, shiny leaves. This is our third autumn at Walla Walla College, so I know it's the time of year to begin battening down the hatches against the cold winter blasts that are gathering to launch their yearly offensive on us. It means that someone from the college grounds crew will eventually come and rake up all these beautiful, golden leaves.

It also means that I should begin putting plastic sheets on the windows to help blunt the effects of the shrill eastern Washington winds. How well I remember our first winter here, when it snowed eighteen inches and the temperature dropped to fifteen degrees below zero for a week. "This is really unusual," the locals said. Ha! I don't believe them anymore. And since I'm a student, it means spending my Sundays holed up in the corner of my bedroom that I euphemistically call my "study"—which my family, however, refers to as my "cave."

But studying and taping shrink-wrap to the windowsills are the last things I want to do on this particular fall weekend.

Now, don't get me wrong; I'm not afraid of work. And I do understand that we need those "storm windows" to help keep our winter heat bill somewhere down in the range of orthodontia payments. I also know that if I get behind in my schoolwork, I'll be digging myself out of the hole for weeks.

But I have the urge to do something totally irrational and irresponsible. I want to go out and drive through miles of sloppy mud on bumpy forest roads and then walk through the cold, wet brush. The pull is so strong that I can't concentrate on my studies. And I know it isn't going to happen—my little Mazda GLC wagon can barely negotiate the speed bumps in the local K-Mart parking lot, let alone plow through the mucky ruts I'm being drawn to. I know that the best way to get sick and miss a ton of school is to leave my warm, dry, cozy bungalow and get cold and wet from head to toe. Yes, my mind is clear on the subject, but my heart doesn't care.

Where has this nutty notion come from? I'm on track to graduate *cum laude*, so obviously, I'm smart enough to know better. Then it hits me. I want to get outdoors, but I don't want to go on a stroll down a hiking trail. I want to tromp in the brush. I want to find a deer path—the kind where apparently very short, scrawny deer squeeze through the scrubby vine maple (which we affectionately call "greasewood," among other, unprintable adjectives) in some sort of maze that baby fawns use to play hide-and-go-seek with their frantic mothers. I want to have someone drop me off on the bottom of a draw so I can trudge up it (as stealthily as a Nez Perce brave, of course) to the road at the top. It's what I did every October during my formative years.

I am crazy.

At least, that's what I thought when the urge first hit me. "Why should I want to do that?" I wondered. I didn't even really like it when I did it.

Better than a dog

You see, in my family I was the "dog" when hunting season came around. My older brothers (whom I idolized) were happy to drag me along on their hunting excursions. They would drop me off at the bottom of a draw and tell me to wait five minutes for them to drive to the top of the ravine. Then I would plod up through the woods, chasing any unsuspecting deer toward them.

I was, in fact, better than a dog. A dog couldn't read a watch to know when the five minutes were up and enter the draw at the exact moment when my brothers were in place on the other side. And a dog wouldn't intentionally drive the deer toward my waiting brothers with their 30-06 rifles and their high-power scopes. A dumb dog would just chase the deer all over creation.

I was a smart dog!

Or so I thought. When my wife learned about this, she said, "I can't believe you went through that brush where your brothers could have shot you!" I guess a woman could never understand how wonderful it is for a young boy to be with his big brothers, even when they are taking full advantage of that blind devotion.

Now that I think about it, while I didn't particularly enjoy being my brothers' hunting dog, doing it became a part of me. After a few years, I really looked forward to getting outdoors from late September to mid-November.

Until the opening day of hunting season right after my fourteenth birthday I hadn't known what it was like to get up at four o'clock in the morning. But that day a skinny teenager traveled down that rite of passage toward adulthood. I was to kill something and eat it!

Oh, how I didn't want to get out of my warm bed that morning. Was it really time to get up? I thought I'd just gone to sleep about fifteen minutes before. I guess what got me up was the notion that my brothers were taking me with them. I was now included in their world. I had graduated to a higher level of maturity. I was a regular guy.

I pulled on my new, freshly oiled hunting boots. I took off the hanger my red plaid hunting jacket that was never quite warm enough but was the right color to keep other hunters from shooting me instead of the deer I was chasing. At least *my mom* considered my safety; she bought that jacket for me.

And there in the kitchen was the smell of four in the morning—coffee! Mom and Dad had never let me drink real black coffee before. This was the sign of adulthood. There's something about drinking steaming black sludge with your older brothers before daylight that makes a boy feel like a man! I even got to pour some in my shiny new, metal (not plastic) thermos jug to take along for the trip.

We arrived at the gated entrance to the timber-company land before sunrise, the second vehicle in the line. A couple of the others in our group took the time till the gate opened to catch up on a bit of the sleep they'd missed the night before. Not me. My nerves allowed me no rest—just more time to fidget and to wonder if I'd remembered everything. Had I packed my ammo? Yes, it's still where it was two minutes ago. Hunting knife? Check. Deer tag? Check. Safety engaged on the gun? Check—but if I don't quit fiddling with it, I'm liable to blow a hole in the roof of the old station wagon. At least, that's what my brother keeps telling me.

We open fire

The caretaker appeared at the crack of dawn and opened the gate. In a cloud of exhaust and dust, dozens of truckloads of hunters raced up the road, each with a particular destination and plan of attack in mind. By the time the sun rose over the Calapooya Mountains in the east, gunfire roared through the clear-cut canyons of the Mosby Creek drainage. An hour or two later, we spotted a half-dozen deer walking along an open path a hundred yards above the road. Even before we were all out of the wagon, someone had opened fire. In a matter of seconds, everyone was firing up the hill. I was the last one out. I pulled the rifle to my shoulder and eyeballed the front sight. Lowering the pin of the front sight into the notch of the rear sight I saw, not the deer I was looking for, but the hunters in my group moving up the hill to find their prey. Having graduated from the hunter's safety course that summer, I decided not to shoot.

In fact, I never fired a shot that day. One member of our group bagged a forked horn in that first onslaught of bullets. I remember seeing how small the animal really was, about the size of a large dog. I mentally measured the tiny antlers and thought, *He must be a teenage deer. Would his mother miss him?*

Out came the knives, and the victorious hunter prepared the deer for the trip home. The sight and smell of deer blood and entrails imprinted itself in my mind. I think it was then I realized that I liked hunting but not killing. I certainly wasn't enamored with the gutting and butchering part!

What an exhilarating feeling to come home with a deer strapped onto the car's hood. Townspeople stopped and pointed as we drove by. Of course, we took the long way through town, with a few extra detours thrown in for good measure.

Then came the best part: We hung our wet clothes around the woodstove to dry and enjoyed hot drinks while we talked about the ones that got away. "There was that four-point I saw right before he ducked into the brush—though I'm sure he had five spikes on one side."

Yes, we could relive a successful expedition. I was now a hunter, a real man, on par with my older brothers and their friends. I was one of the guys!

Hunting became a yearly autumn ritual for me. Whether I went with my brothers or my dad or my own friends or even by myself, that crisp, damp fall air invigorated my lungs. And the fiery red leaves of the vine maples standing out against the green fir backdrop reminded me every year that this is where I belong; this is where I became one of the guys.

Even after I grew up and quit being my brothers' hunting dog, every fall, rain or shine, I tromped through the brush. Though I eventually became accustomed to the killing and butchering part of the ritual, I was never a very good hunter. But come October, I felt drawn to become one with the mud and the rain and the vine-maple jungles.

Then something changed all that. Or so I thought.

I became a Seventh-day Adventist Christian. A vegetarian Seventh-day Adventist Christian. A Seventh-day Adventist Christian who exchanged the word *Sabbath* for *Saturday*. (Opening day of hunting season, by the way, is always on a Saturday.) I became a totally-trusting-in-the-angels-of-God-so-I-don't-even-need-a-gun-for-protection-anymore Seventh-day Adventist Christian. I didn't eat Bambi's mother anymore, and I had no other use for guns. Deer hunting and all the emotional trappings that the ritual entailed were no longer a part of my life. I moved on to an even higher level of maturity—until that urge came on that Sunday in October at

Walla Walla College. What could I do about that urge? Would it go away if I just ignored it? And then I wondered, did becoming a Seventh-day Adventist Christian mean that I was no longer one of the guys? Was the twenty-eighth fundamental belief of Seventh-day Adventism to which I agreed on my baptism day that I must discard all vestiges of "guyness"?

And so I came face to face with an unexpected identity crisis. I don't hunt—but I want to hunt because it's what I've always done—but I don't want to hunt because I don't need to since I now only eat things that never had a mother and senseless killing actually conflicts with my newfound belief system. How can I satisfy this urge and remain true to my faith?

I am a Seventh-day Adventist, a card-carrying member of God's remnant church. I am one of the angels who proclaim the last three messages of warning to a dying world. But I'm also still just a guy from a little town in Oregon. Can I be a Seventh-day Adventist and still be a regular guy? And if so, what does it mean to be a Seventh-day Adventist Christian guy?

For Personal Reflection

- What's your story? Think back on when and how you met Jesus and began following Him.

- What was your life like before you followed Jesus?

- What is life like now that you are a part of His family?

CHAPTER 2

What Planet Are Guys From Anyway?

Why do I use the term *guys* rather than *men*? Well, because guys are different animals than men. Please excuse me for a moment while I make some overly generalized and possibly sexist observations:

- Women are from Venus; men are from Mars; guys are from Pluto. Not the former planet, the goofy-looking hound dog in Disney cartoons.
- If you ask a woman what is her favorite holiday, she will probably say a birthday or an anniversary or Valentine's Day or Christmas. These are all relational events that involve discovering new depths of insight about who she is in relation to the people who are most important in her life. If you ask a man what is his favorite holiday, he will probably say Memorial Day or Independence Day or Labor Day. These holidays relate to meaningful events that help a man reflect on his place in society and in history as a whole. If you ask a guy what is his favorite holiday, he will say Super Bowl Sunday or the day they run

the Indianapolis 500. These events involve yelling things and eating things and drinking things and spilling things with other like-minded creatures.

• When I tell a woman that I used to own a 1968 Z-28 Camaro, she wants to know what color it was. A man wants to know the compression ratio and what kind of gas mileage it got. A guy wants to know, "Where is it? Can I drive it? What on earth possessed you to get rid of it?"

• A woman learns to drive from her father (usually a man). A man takes driver's education classes. A guy learns driving skills on dirt bikes, quads, jeeps, or tractors—often well before he is of legal driving age.

• Last week I saw a guy-in-training—my neighbor's five-year-old son went ripping down the street on a pocket rocket. Not the sidewalk, mind you—the street. (Of course, I'm not recommending that five-year-olds do this. I'm just telling you what he did.) His dad, of course, is a guy. And if you don't know what a pocket rocket is, you probably aren't.

• A woman drives a Toyota Camry. A man drives a Toyota Tundra. A guy drives a 1972 Toyota Land Cruiser J-4 with both the original metal top and a canvas top for summertime and a 327 Chevy engine conversion. And it still runs great!

• A woman learns parenting skills from watching Oprah. A man learns parenting skills from Dr. Phil. A guy learns parenting skills from Tim "the Toolman" Taylor.

• An impulse purchase for a woman is scented votive candles. An impulse purchase for a man is a new fly rod. An impulse purchase for a guy is the old Ford pickup down the street "because I need it for the parts."

- A woman's shopping list is mostly food and household items. A man's shopping list is mostly repair and maintenance items for the home. A guy's shopping list is in his head—"I know there's something I was supposed to get here. Oh well, might as well get some ammo for the 30-06 while I'm here."

- A woman "doesn't get" football. A man can diagram all the X's and O's. A guy knows immediately that the safety is going to blitz the quarterback so he'd better call an audible and dump a quick pass to the tailback. When my daughter was three years old, she was well on her way to being quite a guy. She'd come and watch what she called "knock 'em down" with her dad. That girl got football!—that is, until she discovered horsies and dollies and the cutest little pink ballerina dress you ever saw.

- A woman enjoys listening to Dr. Laura. A man listens either to "All Things Considered" or Rush Limbaugh. A guy knows the real names of the "Car Talk" hosts, Click and Clack, the Tappet Brothers.

- A woman's bumper sticker says, "I'm Pro-Life and I Vote." A man's bumper sticker says, "Semper Fi." A guy's bumper sticker says, "On the Seventh Day God Went Four-Wheeling."

- In the church, a woman is often a deaconess, a greeter, or a children's Sabbath School teacher. A man is an elder. A guy is a deacon.

- Women attend women's retreats. Men attend Promise Keepers rallies. Guys watch sporting events together.

- When a loved one is sick, a woman grieves because a vital part of her life is suffering. A man grieves because it is the rational emotional response that leads to personal growth and healing. A guy grieves over sick loved ones because he can't fix them.

Sorry for the overly simplistic generalizations, but I'm hoping you can see that life for guys is different than for anyone else. The important thing to remember is that God created guys for a special purpose. However, that purpose isn't always readily obvious.

So back to my questions: Is it possible to be a Seventh-day Adventist Christian guy? And if so, what does he look like and how does spirituality work in his life? As I'll discuss later, spirituality for guys often involves simply what works and what doesn't work.

Why address spiritual issues for guys? I don't know how it is at your local Adventist Book Center, but mine has a large section on women's ministry topics. There are devotional books for women, Bibles for women, emotional healing books for women, nutrition books for women, books on family life, and books on how to set proper boundaries in a loving Christian way.

For years, my local Adventist Book Center didn't have a men's ministry section. Now there are a few books for men at the end of a shelf. But those books don't do much for guys. Most guys think that the books for men were actually written by women for women. They think those books tell how to change your pig of a husband (a guy) into Prince Charming (used to be a guy but is now an unrecognizable species).

OK, I'll admit that there are some great books out there written by men for men—but guys don't read those books. There usually aren't enough pictures, and the words in the psychological study evaluations and reports are too big. Those books are helpful for men who want to be better men. Guys don't necessarily want to change. They want to be accepted for who God created them to be. But guys often struggle in their spirituality because they feel that their "guy-ness" is somehow un-Christian. I haven't found much written on this topic because either (A) most guys don't get into writing books, or (B) nobody buys these books so publishers won't print them. I can't help B, but I can do something about A; hence this book.

Guys and "men's retreats"

A while back, I was invited to speak at a Seventh-day Adventist men's retreat, and I discovered why these retreats are so uncommon. A few days before the weekend, the organizer called and said he was having a hard time getting men to commit to coming. I couldn't imagine why. My theme for the weekend was "Spirituality and the Average Guy." I thought it was a great topic that every guy would love to check out.

It wasn't the topic that was the problem. It was the whole concept of a men's retreat. The only frame of reference these men had for what a men's retreat would be is what they'd heard from their wives who had attended women's retreats. They envisioned sessions involving hours of sitting in a circle and tossing a football to each other and having to share their deepest, innermost feelings when they caught the football. Of course, these guys ran like cockroaches under a floodlight at the thought. They don't have deep innermost feelings and can't pretend they do because they don't even have the slightest idea how to make up something that sounds plausible!

A recent Hagar the Horrible cartoon sums up the whole situation. Hagar and Helga are sitting together. Helga is knitting and glancing at Hagar. He's simply sitting there with a benign look on his face. Helga's thought balloon reads, "He looks so innocent, but he's always plotting something. If only I could see inside that diabolical mind of his." Hagar's thought balloon is empty.*

Guys really do prefer to keep life as simple and uncomplicated as possible!

Many non-Christian guys often see spirituality as weak—something women do. "If you turn to Christ, there must be something wrong with you. What's the matter? Are you some wimp who can't take care of himself? If you were a real man, you wouldn't need God." That view can even permeate the attitudes of truly converted Christian guys.

The organizers of the retreat and I decided that it was time to reclaim the masculine aspect of spirituality. We began by reassuring the guys that no one would be pressured to talk. I came fully prepared to do all the talking, but I didn't actually have to. Once these men recognized that God valued them just the way they are, that they didn't need to remake themselves or pretend to be something they aren't, they felt free to open up and really explore the sanctity of being guys for God.

I understand that most guys don't realize that they really do have deep, innermost feelings. We want to get up in the morning, go to work, do our best, and provide for our families. We love our families, though we don't often know how to say it. But we do love them, and we really do expect that our loved ones will know that and accept it. We really do love God too, but please don't ask us to share in Sabbath School how that love affects us personally. We often experience and share the impact of God's love in practical, nonverbal ways.

So we didn't get into deeply emotional, group-sharing sessions at that men's retreat. We talked about camping and going to work and church and the practical ways we show that we love our families and love God. And the guys loved it.

And I believe that's biblical.

For Personal Reflection

- What do you enjoy most about being a guy?

- Most men are a blend of man and guy. What percentage of your personality is guy and what percentage is man?

- Have you ever tried to be something or someone that you are not? Why? What was the result?

---

* Chris Browne, "Hagar the Horrible," Sept. 3, 2004. King Features Syndicate.

CHAPTER 3

If I Lose My Job, Who Am I?

One of the first big challenges I faced as a newly baptized Seventh-day Adventist came when I needed to go job hunting. I was a welder in a boxcar repair shop at a local railroad at the time, but work was slowing down. The stagnant economy of the early 1980s meant that fewer goods were being shipped by rail, which meant that fewer boxcars were being banged up by careless forklift operators, which meant that fewer boxcars needing repair came into our shop. Our concern grew as we watched the line of cars in the yard shrink daily.

Sabbath keeping wasn't an issue for me at my shop—we never worked Saturdays. In fact, the bosses appreciated my newfound beliefs because of the lifestyle changes that came with my conversion. To be blunt, I wasn't calling in sick from hangovers or showing up at work stone drunk anymore!

Now, however, I had to make a serious effort to find new employment, if only to qualify for weekly unemployment benefits. I went to a small, gypo logging outfit. Maybe they needed a welder to fix broken equipment. More likely I would be a "gofer"—an unskilled laborer to "gofer this and gofer that." I was young, strong, and willing.

The foreman looked like my kind of a guy. He sort of reminded me of my dad: graying around the temples, a bit of a southern drawl, wearing work boots and overalls—the kind of adult I'd grown up around, and typical of the foremen I had worked for during the previous eight years.

I sat down on the old beat-up couch in the little trailer that served as the office for this outfit and began filling out the paperwork. The employment application was simple, straightforward, and asked the question I knew would come: "Is there any time that you cannot work?" I answered, "Yes," and in the explanation box I wrote, "I am a Seventh-day Adventist, so I won't work from Friday evening at sundown until Saturday evening at sundown."

That shouldn't have posed a problem for this company, but apparently it did for the foreman. "You one of them Seventh-day Advents?" he asked without looking up from the application.

"Sure am," I replied, hoping for the chance to tell him about what God had done for me, and how I would be an honest, conscientious employee.

"Sorry," he said as he casually dropped my paperwork into the chewing-tobacco-stained wastebasket by the beat-up desk. "Don't need no Seventh-day Advents here."

I had no chance to show him that I could do the work. No chance to show that I could fit in well with his crew. No chance to show that a "Seventh-day Advent" could also be just one of the guys. It seemed so unfair. But it was one of the ways my life differed because of my new identity. Maybe my status as a Seventh-day Adventist Christian negated my status as a regular guy. *Just who am I now?* I wondered.

Christian spirituality can create an identity crisis in guys. It affects every aspect of who we are.

Guys fix things

Guys are, by nature, fixers. We know just enough about auto repair, carpentry, plumbing, landscaping, and electronics to be generally useful (though sometimes dangerous). We aren't afraid to tackle a problem. In fact, we often enjoy problems because working on them gives us a chance to hone our troubleshooting skills. Problem-solving gives us a sense of accomplishment, and we have this need to feel self-sufficient.

Madison Avenue advertisers know this. A television commercial for an auto-parts store featured a guy and his Jeep. The Jeep broke down, but the guy said, "I can fix that." He found the right part at this store and fixed his Jeep. Then he wanted to customize it, so he said, "I can fix that," and found all kinds of cool accessories at this store. The last part of the commercial pictures the beautiful, tricked-out Jeep cruising down the road and the guy saying, "The only problem now is that my girlfriend is mad at me for spending so much time with my Jeep." It ends with him saying, "But I can fix that." We even see relationship problems as things we can fix.

I had a great day yesterday. The plug on my 12-volt cooler burnt up. Since I'm living in my old tent trailer in the woods right now, this is a big problem. I need this cooler to survive, just like the miners in days of old! I had to figure out how to take the old plug off the cord and determine which lead is positive and which is the ground. Next, I had to drive into town and hunt through department stores and auto-parts stores until I found a replacement plug. I have a toolbox but no soldering iron, so I used a butane lighter to melt the solder off the old plug. Then I pinched the cord wires onto the new plug with my old, worn pliers and *voilá!* my butter won't melt and my eggs won't spoil. It was the highlight of my day. I am self-sufficient, even in these primitive conditions!

However, Christians can't be self-sufficient. They have to give up control to Jesus. To a guy, that means, "You can't fix everything." That's hard for a guy to take. So, when Jesus says, " 'Apart from me you can do nothing,' " (John 15:5), it's not an issue of pride; it's like He's sticking in a dagger and ripping out the identity of the average guy—an identity that's been instilled in us from birth. Our society—our parents, our friends, our educators—all teach guys to be providers and fixers and caretakers. To be less than that is an affront to our manhood. To give up that control erodes the foundation of our self-worth.

Christian guys have to learn that our self-worth comes from another source, outside of ourselves. But that goes against everything we've ever known about ourselves and the environment we live in.

Seventh-day Adventist Christian guys find this stumbling block especially challenging. The Sabbath, by its very nature, reminds us every week that we can't do it all: " 'Six days you shall labor and do all your work, but the seventh day is a Sabbath to the LORD your God. On it you shall not do any work' " (Exodus 20:9, 10). Guys feel the need to be productive, whether it is at work or around the house. Now we are told that we can do our very best for six days, but it's never good enough. God tells us to stop for this one day and hear Jesus say, " 'My grace is sufficient for you, for my power is made perfect in weakness' " (2 Corinthians 12:9). We appreciate the grace of our Lord Jesus Christ, but is it ever hard to let go of our self-sufficiency!

"Sensitive males"?

Another identity issue arose back in the early 1990s. I remember it as the "sensitive male" movement. This movement seemed to be especially prominent in Christian groups. I'm sure that the motives behind it were good, but guys heard it as "If you are a man, you are an insensitive brute who needs to be refined." From this movement arose the notion that because we were now Christians, people expected us to open up more about our inner feelings and rid ourselves of everything we'd ever been taught about what it means to be a man. Put simply, it scared us!

We guys feel that we are already sensitive to our loved ones—we just don't always know how to express it. The whole sensitive-male notion seemed to tell us that we were failures. We knew we weren't failures, but we didn't always have the right words to win the argument. Later, we'll look at practical ways guys can express their love to their families in true guy language.

Men who convert to Christianity later in life can experience an identity crisis in their social lives. These are not always bad changes. If your social life revolved around sitting at a bar after work, then you needed a change. But the sentiment of the theme song of a popular TV sitcom rings true for many guys: "Sometimes you want to go where everybody knows your name and they're always glad you came."* Unfortunately, many guys find that bars provide a camaraderie, understanding, and acceptance of each other that is hard to find elsewhere. People there know your joys and struggles and how much you paid for your motorcycle. Some guys tell their bartender things that they'd never say to their wife. But the bar scene is not a wholesome environment for God's people. If your social life centered on unwholesome activities in unsavory places, then a change was certainly in order.

Many times our commitment to Christ demands that we divorce ourselves from unhealthy peer influences. But that change doesn't necessarily come easily. We often feel like traitors to our old friends, some of whom stood by us in hard times. Now they don't understand our lifestyle changes. Old friends can feel that when we turned away from that old lifestyle, we were abandoning them as well. What an identity crisis! We may still love the people, but we just can't associate with them.

Our identity is often expressed in our entertainment choices. What you read, the type of music you listen to, and the TV shows you watch indicate who you are. My dad enjoyed watching *The Grand Ol' Opry, The Beverly Hillbillies,* and *Hee Haw.* Those choices tell you something about who he was. He grew up playing hillbilly bluegrass guitar and fiddle in the Ozarks. I was involved in the rock music industry of the 1960s and 1970s. (OK, I was the bass player in several loud garage bands!) That reveals a bit about my previous identity, and you can also guess the kinds of cultural clashes my dad and I experienced!

Randy, the lead singer in my rock band, came over one evening during the time my wife and I were going through our conversion transformation. Typically, I would have a stack of *Guitar Player* and *Rolling Stone* magazines in the living room. This evening, Randy picked up my *Signs of the Times®* magazine from the coffee table. He saw the cover, which featured an illustration of the earth on fire with the caption "How Will It End?" At that moment, our relationship changed. Randy said something to the effect of "You don't really believe this garbage, do you?" He was really saying, "You are different. You're not the same person I used to know." My identity had changed; my choice of reading material revealed that, and it affected my social relationships.

Randy got drunk and wrapped his car around a tree a few years later, and my problem-solving nature took a big hit. I had solved the big problem in my life: Jesus is the answer to all my problems. As much as I had wanted to share the good news about Jesus with Randy, he didn't want to hear it. But I couldn't help Randy solve his problems. I realize that Randy made his own choices in life and I can't be responsible for his death, but it still hurts to know that I had the solution for Randy, yet I couldn't fix him. Yeah, guys really do grieve deeply.

However, the changes that challenge our sense of identity have a positive side. I'm still alive. I greatly enjoy life with my loving wife and kids, and I'm a first-time grandpappy to an adorable little girl. Life has never been better for me. I could just as easily have died young and miserable like Randy. It helps to keep things in perspective while we sort through these things.

"Watch your language"

Changes in how you relate to co-worker guys also affect your identity. Maybe you used to be the one to tell the latest off-color joke in the break room. Now, not only do you not tell them, but your face turns seven different shades of crimson when you hear them. The change affects your relationships at work and can cause an identity crisis. Just who are you in the workplace now?

I heard a Christian attorney say that Christians can now sue their employers to force co-workers to clean up their language in the workplace. I have mixed feelings about this. Sure, it's nice not to have to hear your Lord's name used as a cuss word, but would you really want to sue for that benefit? Think about the contentious us-against-them atmosphere that could create. How you endure foul language is a personal choice for each Christian in the workplace, but it also illustrates the kind of dilemmas guys face at work.

Often, a guy's occupation defines his identity. When I learned that my welding job was disappearing and that I would have to learn a new trade since the market was flooded with out-of-work welders, I felt intense internal turmoil. My image of myself was as challenged as it would have been if someone had cut off my nose. A vital part of what made me who I am was forcefully removed from my life. I was a welder—my world involved getting up at a certain time and driving to a certain shop and working with a certain crew. I could cope with changing shops and crews, but changing vocations? Welding was infused into every fiber of my being.

I know of new Seventh-day Adventist Christian guys who had to change jobs because of moral conflicts and Sabbath conflicts. Some were bartenders. Others were card dealers in casinos. One was a farmer who grew hops for brewing beer. It was his most lucrative crop. Sabbath-keepers often face a crisis when their new religious convictions conflict with their job—usually because their job requires them to work on Sabbath.

Other issues for Seventh-day Adventist Christian guys involve our healthy lifestyle—a great benefit that God has given us in His Word, but a challenge to our identity as guys. Vegetarianism is the best diet for a healthy lifestyle, but what does that do to a hunter? What do you do when your buddies invite you over for a steak or when all your old friends want you to join them at the local sports bar to watch Monday Night Football?

What if Saturday used to be the day on which you took your family out to the lake for a barbecue? Now the day is Sabbath, and you take your family to church and a potluck. This is a positive change, but it affects who a guy is.

I believe that Adventism has the greatest message of hope and salvation for the world and there is no better identity for a guy than to be a Seventh-day Adventist Christian. It just takes some time to sort out the personal identity issues involved in being a Seventh-day Adventist Christian guy.

We are, in fact, in great company. In the next chapter, we'll see some biblical examples of regular guys.

For Personal Reflection

- What areas in your life have caused conflicts between your sense of manhood and your faith?

- How have you resolved these conflicts?

- Are any still unresolved?

---

* Theme song from the TV show *Cheers*.

CHAPTER 4

Yes, There Really Are Guys in the Bible

A museum near the Kibbutz Ginosar in northern Israel, alongside the Sea of Galilee, features an incredible find. One dry summer about twenty years ago, the water level of the Sea of Galilee dropped, exposing lakebed that was usually under water. In the mud on this new shoreline, a beachcomber made a startling discovery—a boat that turned out to be about two thousand years old. The waterlogged wood hull had the consistency of wet cardboard, so archaeologists excavated it with great care and then transported it to a climate-controlled environment. Today, the museum conservators keep the fragile frame and hull in water to preserve it from decomposition.

Archaeologists believe this craft is a typical Galilean fishing boat from the first century A.D. It's not very big. It actually looks more like a canoe than a fishing boat.

The day before I saw this boat, I stood along the shores of Galilee in a driving rainstorm. I wanted to see how Galilean rainstorms compare to rain back home in Oregon. (If you don't understand why I would do this, you just need to know that this is a guy thing to do.) The Galilean rainstorm was impressive! The Sea of Galilee is about the size of Oregon's Crater Lake, but it seems to generate its own weather. Warm, damp air from the Mediterranean Sea drifts inland, collides with the cool air over Galilee, and *boom!*—you have an instant storm, complete with wind and waves that rival the Pacific Coast storms I'm used to.

My first thought when I saw that ancient boat was *Peter, James, and John fished from a boat like this? They were some pretty rugged guys!* I could picture those massive waves tossing this boat about as if it were a teacup. Imagine the strength and skill it would take to guide this canoe through a Galilean storm. They had no weather channel on a short-wave radio to warn them of approaching squalls. They had no GPS trackers to guide them into safe harbors when the dense clouds closed in on them. They had no inboard or outboard motor to power them through the wind and over the waves. They rowed and prayed!

Later on the same day that our group visited the first-century boat museum, we took a boat ride on Galilee's waters in a twentieth-century boat. The boatman showed us Peter, James, and John's fishing technique, which Galilean fishermen still use today. With a motion like the one you'd use to throw a Frisbee, he flung a round net out into the water. The ten-foot net had weights attached to the hemmed edge and a cord tied to the center. As the net descended into the murky depths of the sea, it gathered fish. When the cord in the center of the net drew tight, the weights on the edge of the net continued down until the net had fully enclosed the fish. Then the fisherman began pulling the net up. As I watched the demonstration, I envisioned the massive arms and the upper-body strength first-century fishermen must have had to do this several times a day, day in and day out, week after week, for a lifetime.

Rugged characters

The Bible gives us some clues about the ruggedness of those disciples' characters. James and John wanted to call down fire from heaven and nuke a whole village because someone hurt their feelings (Luke 9:54, 55). Jesus revealed a bit of His sense of humor when He called them "sons of thunder."

Peter promised to defend Jesus to the death, and he carried a sword to prove it. Sure enough, when the mob came to arrest Jesus in the Garden of Gethsemane, Peter tried to whack off Malchus's head with that sword. And later that night, when some of the gawkers in Caiphus's courtyard accused him of being a follower of Jesus, he cursed like the sailor he was deep down in his heart.

Come to think of it, Peter, James, and John were just like several of the guys I grew up with. Yet, under the influence of the Holy Spirit, these men were transformed; they were still guys, but after their conversion experience, they were sanctified guys.

John's brother James went, apparently meekly, to his death (see Acts 12). There is no record of this "son of thunder" fighting or cursing the injustice. The man who wanted to incinerate an entire village for wounding his pride went to his death as a lamb led to slaughter. He emulated the example of his Lord, who, "as a sheep before her shearers is silent, so he did not open his mouth" (Isaiah 53:7).

Acts 12 pictures Peter sleeping soundly in prison too. He knew that the next morning he would face the same fate as James, yet he didn't fight or curse. Could you sleep if you knew that the next day you faced execution at the whim of a corrupt ruler? Peter slept the sound sleep of someone who, filled with God's Holy Spirit, rests in the care of Jesus.

Later, this same Peter wrote, "Husbands . . . be considerate as you live with your wives" (1 Peter 3:7). These words are from a guy, no less! Who needs all that "sensitive male" haranguing when the Holy Spirit can transform a rough guy like Peter into a considerate husband who is at peace with the world?

John, the other "son of thunder," wrote the Gospel that bears his name—the biblical book known by many as "the Gospel of love." In his first epistle, he wrote, "This is the message you heard from the beginning: We should love one another. . . . Dear friends, since God so loved us, we also ought to love one another. . . . We love because he first loved us" (1 John 3:11; 4:11, 19). When a "son of thunder" type of guy tells other guys to "love one another," we ought to sit up and take notice!

Paul was a guy. He had a regular job like you and me—he was a tentmaker. Now, imagine making tents in Paul's day. He had no sewing machines. He had no light, synthetic materials. He sewed animal skins by hand. You think you're tough? Go skin some animals and sew their hides into a tent—one that you personally would live in—by hand. When I go backpacking, I carry a tent that weighs three and a half pounds. Imagine lugging around a hundred square yards of rolled-up camel hide. Paul was a real tough guy, yet at the end of his life he said, "I am already being poured out like a drink offering" (2 Timothy 4:6). He humbly offered himself as a sacrifice for the sake of the gospel.

Job was a guy. He was a sheep rancher who owned three thousand camels. Camels were the heavy haulers of the day, so Job was in the trucking business. He also had five hundred yoke of oxen, so he was in the farm-implements industry. In addition, he had five hundred donkeys. Donkeys were personal transportation, so he ran a used-car lot. He also had an active prayer and devotional life and ministered to his family as the priest of his household.

David, a guy, was a "man after God's own heart." He was a soldier who served his time in the military, like many regular guys today. He also wrote some of the most beautiful and powerful poetry the world has ever known. Many of our most popular hymns and choruses today are direct quotes from David's pen. Want to see a combination of rugged guy and sensitive male? Look at David.

Prime minister of an empire

Daniel was tough. He would rather die than violate God's health laws. He risked his life to go before Nebuchadnezzar and reveal the contents and interpretation of a dream. Nebuchadnezzar made Daniel the prime minister of Babylon, the most powerful nation on earth at the time. A modern-day position comparable to that which Daniel held is U.S. secretary of state.

Daniel had to make tough decisions in the day-to-day operation of the Babylonian dynasty. He plainly told King Belshazzar that he was weighed in the balances and found wanting and that God had given Babylon to the Medes and Persians. Yet this tough-as-nails guy took time out to have devotions morning, noon, and night. Because Daniel prayed three times a day, he was convicted of a capital offense and sentenced to death by hungry lions. Daniel knew that his toughness wouldn't save him from the lions. He confessed, " 'My God sent his angel, and he shut the mouths of the lions' " (Daniel 6:22). See what a life of devotion to God can do for rough and rugged guys?

The Bible is full of regular guys like you and me. Moses spent forty years living in the wilderness as a sheep herder. Gideon ran a farm. Nehemiah was a royal taster for King

Artaxerxes. Imagine the courage it took to sample wine before each meal and wonder if this was the time someone had decided to poison the king!

Stephen, one of the original deacons, preached one of the most eloquent sermons in Scripture as he was facing death. A centurion—a real guy's guy in first-century Rome—expressed his faith that Jesus could just speak the word and heal his servant (see Luke 7:1–10). Another centurion saw the way Jesus died and proclaimed, " 'Surely he was the Son of God!' " (Matthew 27:54). And after a Bible study from Peter, the centurion Cornelius and his entire household were baptized. Imagine any of these centurions explaining to his regiment commander that he now followed an itinerant rabbi from Judah whom Rome had crucified. That took some real guts!

Probably the best example of a Bible guy is Jesus. He was a carpenter. Most carpenters that I know of today are guys. But in terms of rugged toughness, my carpenter friends would have a hard time matching the work Jesus did. Carpenters in His day often provided their own raw materials. That meant Jesus had to fell trees, so He was a logger. He would mill the log and plane it into useable boards, so He was a mill worker. He would craft it into a table or a chair, so He was a furniture maker. He probably did it from a design He thought up, so He was also a draftsman. And He did it all with hand tools— let's see today's carpenters do all that!

We often see Jesus portrayed in artwork and movies as some scrawny, emaciated little guy who seems likely to break in the slightest wind. I've worked in a mill and done enough carpentry to know better. Jesus was no wimp.

Guys who set chokers and pull boards off a green chain and carry four-by-eight sheets of plywood up onto a roof have to be pretty tough. Jesus would fit right in working on any crew I've been on. His hands were blistered and calloused from His work. He would carry His end of the load, and then He'd hang out with the guys after work. He was even chastised by the "religious people" for eating with "sinners" (see Matthew 9:11). When those "religious people" said "sinners," they were talking about regular people, like you and me and our loved ones.

The Bible is full of Spirit-filled guys. Now it's time to see how spirituality works in the life of a Seventh-day Adventist guy.

For Personal Reflection

- Which Bible guy do you most admire? Why?
- Which Bible guy would you invite over to do the guy activity you enjoy most, like watching the Super Bowl or Indy 500?
- Which Bible guy would you want to help fix your car?

CHAPTER 5

How to Be a Good Bible-type Guy

I made a crack earlier about how guys need pictures for concepts to become clear to them. There's an element of truth in that statement. We like things spelled out in clear, concrete (there's a guy image for you) terms.

Guys appreciate plain, straightforward communication. Don't talk to us in riddles or codes. If people tell us Yes but expect that we will read their body language or facial expressions as a No, they're asking for trouble. We take what people say at face value and believe in plain, simple communication. I'll discuss some ways for guys to expand their communication abilities in a later chapter because we can always grow in this area. And it's not as painful as you think!

Jesus was a master communicator. Sure, He was a guy, but He also knew how to use parables to confound those who were opposed to Him. Some people love to decipher His riddles. His disciples were not among those people—they were all guys, remember? His disciples wanted Him to speak plainly and were often frustrated by His "figures of speech" (see John 16:17–30).

Jesus was really speaking to a guy's heart when He said, " 'Let your "Yes" be "Yes" and your "No" be No" ' " (Matthew 5:37). Guys respond to plain talk with no mind games or hidden agendas. That's why I see Galatians 5:16–23 as a valuable passage for guys. It's as plain and straightforward as any text of Scripture. It is simply two lists, a list of good things and a list of bad things. We guys work best with lists: Tell us what to do and we'll do it; tell us what not to do and we won't.

Some of the elements in Galatians 5:16–23 create word pictures in our minds. This too is good because many of us are visual thinkers. Don't write out directions—draw us a map. We got this way playing football as kids, when the quarterback would draw a hook-and-go pattern in the dirt and we'd run it just as we'd seen it. Galatians 5:16–23 uses concrete word pictures that guys can understand. It goes like this:

> Live by the Spirit, and you will not gratify the desires of the sinful nature. For the sinful nature desires what is contrary to the Spirit, and the Spirit what is contrary to the sinful nature. They are in conflict with each other, so that you do not do what you want. But if you are led by the Spirit, you are not under law.
>
> The acts of the sinful nature are obvious: sexual immorality, impurity and debauchery; idolatry and witchcraft; hatred, discord, jealousy, fits of rage, selfish ambition, dissensions, orgies, and the like. I warn you, as I did before, that those who live like this will not inherit the kingdom of God.
>
> But the fruit of the Spirit is love, joy, peace, patience, kindness, goodness, faithfulness, gentleness and self-control. Against such things there is no law.

This passage lays out for us a problem and a solution, isn't that great? The message to guys is simply this: If you want to do what's right, you need the Holy Spirit.

Unfortunately, we often know exactly what the bad things look like. Even more unfortunate is the fact that we can remember clearly times when we've done them. We can recall either when we've thrown one of those "fits of rage" Paul wrote about (and wished later that we hadn't) or when we've been at the receiving end of one. So when Paul tells us not to do these things, we know exactly what not to do.

Applying Paul's lists

How do these lists apply to the things that make guys who they are? Well, the lists are less about what your guy interests are than how you go about doing those guy interests. Sure, some interests are incompatible with Christian faith—there's no way to drink and gamble and carouse with women of ill repute in a Spirit-filled way. But we can do many guy activities in harmony with our faith.

Now, here's the hard part for guys: These lists are less about the outward man and more about the inward person. Yes, this is the part where we dig past the shallow exterior life that we guys feel comfortable living and explore our deeper regions. The good news is that you can do this between you and God alone—no group therapy is needed! We'll look at how to let God's Holy Spirit change you from the inside out later. For now, simply ask yourself, Can I do guy things with love? Joy? Peace? Patience? Kindness? Goodness? Faithfulness? Gentleness? Self-control?

John was a real guy. He was a hard worker and knew how to fix things and build things. While he was a high school graduate, he had no college experience; but he did have a level of wisdom that comes from a lifetime of experiencing life's ups and downs—something no college can teach.

The church that John attended was outgrowing its building. When the leaders began the process of deciding whether to plant a new church in the area or build a new, bigger facility, John knew the wise course of action: Plant a new church. He'd seen other churches go through this process, and he knew the results. He felt two smaller churches would have a closer, more family oriented atmosphere than one large church. He also thought the money needed to build a fancy new church could better be spent on church planting and evangelism.

Other church leaders felt differently about the situation, and they decided to build a larger church facility. John had spoken up in the meetings and shared the benefit of his wisdom and experience, but to no avail. The new church was planned, and work was set to begin.

John could easily have continued his opposition to the building program. Everyone knew he didn't agree with it. Enough people had sided with John that they could have left the church and started another in the area. All that, though well intentioned, would have fallen into the category of the first list: discord, dissentions, and factions. John didn't live according to the first list. Instead, he showed up bright and early the first day of construction, his hammer in hand and his nail belt strapped to his waist. John worked as hard as anyone on the new building.

The end of the story goes like this: The new building is beautiful, but the church really hasn't grown much since they completed it. They have nice programs in the facility, but the atmosphere isn't familylike, as it used to be. It turned out almost exactly the way John said it would. However, though many today wish they'd listened more closely to John's counsel, he's never said, "I told you so." The apostle Paul also said, "Love keeps no record of wrongs."

Spirituality for guys is often less about what you do than it is about how you do it. Do you live according to the first list or the second? Everyone involved in the church-building project will always remember that John lived according to the second, Spirit-filled list.

Can you go hunting according to the second list? Some hunters use foul language when their prey slips away. Do you have to use crude language to hunt? No, your lips can be anointed with goodness from above. Some hunters not only go after the big game animal indicated on their tag, but they also shoot at every little chipmunk and tweety bird that moves. As I drive the forest roads around my camp, I can count on one hand the number of road signs that aren't peppered with bullet holes. Do you have to act like Rambo Jr. when you hunt? No, your attitude can be infused with kindness from the Holy Spirit.

Hunting isn't necessarily anti-Christian. Hunting done in the mode of the first list is.

What about hot rods?

Can a Christian guy still enjoy hot rods? Some hot-rod magazines are filled with scantily clad models who probably don't know a fuel injector from a piston ring. But as a Spirit-filled hot-rod enthusiast, you can be like Job, who said, " 'I made a covenant with my eyes not to look lustfully at a girl' " (Job 31:1).

My friend Scott runs his own automotive shop. Many auto shops feature calendars that are chosen not because of the accurate information about today's date but because of the girlie photos. These calendars reveal a lot about the men who work there. Some of these calendars stay up year after year, and not because the guys want to know what day of the week was October 1, 1987. I've seen some shops where the calendars stay up until the photos are so faded that they've almost become decent again. The only photos on the calendars at Scott's shop, however, are of classic cars.

One day I told Scott how much I appreciated the clean, wholesome atmosphere in his shop. I never felt uncomfortable bringing my wife or kids there. He knew immediately what I was getting at. "Oh yeah," he said. "They send me those calendars for free to advertise their products. I immediately toss that garbage in the trash and send them back a letter stating that I won't buy their parts as long as I keep getting that junk from them!"

A Spirit-filled guy can appreciate the automotive arts with a commitment to faithfulness.

OK, now I'll probably step on some toes. Sometimes our guy interests can get out of balance with the rest of our lives. Our priorities should be in an order that looks somewhat like this:

#1. God
#2. Family
#3. Guy things

There, that should be simple enough. Now, ask yourself if this is how you arrange your life. You can tell by comparing how much time and money you invest in each thing. Remember, Jesus—a guy—said, " 'Where your treasure is, there your heart will be also' " (Matthew 6:21).

A woman will feel a twinge of guilt when she treats herself to a box of chocolates, but some guys will unashamedly treat themselves to a new dirt bike "because I need it to relieve the stress of the rat race." Did that indulgence take funds away from the offering plate or food off your table? We guys have to be careful to give God and our families the attention they are due.

Don't worry; you'll still have time to be a guy. Just make sure that you are a kind, gentle, faithful guy for God and a loving family guy first.

For Personal Reflection

- If an independent auditor looked at your budget, how would he list your priorities?

- What evidence do you see in your life of the first list in Galatians?

- What evidence do you see in your life of the second list?

Chapter 6

Don't Just Sit There, Do Something!

One day, during my daily Bible reading, I came across a couple of verses that really puzzled me. The first one is Jeremiah 7:23, " ' "I gave them this command: Obey me, and I will be your God and you will be my people." ' " The second verse is like unto it: " 'I said, "Obey me and do everything I command you, and you will be my people, and I will be your God" ' " (Jeremiah 11:4).

What I read created a great problem in my mind because the process it seemed to describe was backwards from everything I've known about God and His plan for our salvation. Romans 5:8 says, "God demonstrates his own love for us in this: While we were still sinners, Christ died for us." And 1 John 4:19 puts it this way, "We love because he first loved us."

What a theological quandary! The Bible says that God loved us before we ever did anything loving toward Him, and His love is what inspires us to love Him back. But these verses in Jeremiah seem to say that God will not be our God until we obey Him first. What's a guy to do?

As I pondered this seeming contradiction, it struck me that Jeremiah 7:23 and 11:4 are verses for guys. There are two sides to these verses, *do* and then *be*. *Obey* His commands, and then *be* His man. Spirituality for guys often involves *doing* something first; the *being* comes as a result. In other words, we tend to become what we do.

I was a welder before I entered the ministry. But I wasn't born a welder. I became a welder. I learned welding when I got a job in a boxcar repair shop as the cleanup guy. I began by watching how the welders set the power on their machines and how they struck an arc. Sometimes I'd be picking up some scrap around a workstation when one of the welders would ask me to hold a piece of metal while he tacked it in place. Eventually, they just held the metal piece where they wanted it and asked me to tack it in place. But I wasn't a welder yet.

As I immersed myself in the world of welding, I wanted to know more. My friend Dan and I would stay after work, and, using scrap pieces, he'd show me how to weld. Every morning the foreman wondered about the funny-looking creations of scrap held together by some ugly looking globs of weld. I was still not a welder.

Over time, the welds started looking better. Now I could help the repairmen with small beads, and they started showing me their tricks and techniques. And after a few months, I was promoted from cleanup guy to carman. I wasn't a great welder, but I could do the job. Some days I'd face new challenges, but with coaching from the other carmen and a lot of trial and error, I'd master these challenges and move on.

I think it was when I began dreaming in my sleep about how to run a perfect-looking bead on a patch of metal skin on the side of a boxcar that I started considering myself a welder. I had to do the job over and over again before I became what I did. I had to weld and weld and weld *before* I became a welder.

That's how it can be for a guy in his spiritual life. We don't often feel spiritual first and then start doing spiritual things; feeling the presence of God can elude us for months and years. If we wait to feel the presence of the Holy Spirit, we may never move on to living a spiritually disciplined life. A guy often has to do spiritual things first, and then, over time, God begins to take the central role in a guy's life. It's not that God waits for us to be good enough for Him. It's that a change takes place in us because of what we've been doing. We do spiritual things until those spiritual activities change us and become who we are.

Unfortunately, this process holds a danger point for guys. Sometimes a man's whole spiritual life remains in the realm of *doing*. But we can't earn our salvation. At some point we have to accept Jesus, not our works, as our Savior. While we live in the realm of doing, at some point, spirituality has to become our identity—we need to make the move from being a guy who *does* spiritual things to *being* a spiritual guy. But that's the next chapter.

A different kind of spirituality

I never really considered my dad a spiritual guy. I never saw him do things that appeared spiritual. I didn't see him attend church from the day I knew what a church was until the day he died. I never saw him read a Bible or pray. It appeared to me that he had no spirituality whatsoever. This bothered me after I became a Christian. I want to see all of my loved ones in heaven. Dad, however, had passed away eight years before my conversion. I hesitated to consider his eternal condition. I found it best not to think about his fate and to leave it in God's hands.

Through the years, however, I've learned things about my dad that I never knew when he was alive. I knew he was an honest man. I knew that he worked hard and provided for all of our needs, even if he couldn't afford all of our wants. I never saw him drink a drop of alcohol, and I never heard him utter a curse word. What I wasn't aware of were the things he did for others when we weren't around. He did these things quietly, never advertising his good deeds.

When a fellow worker died, Dad took a load of firewood to the family and helped with some gardening and yard work. When my cousin went through a divorce and found herself in the position of being a single mother to two little children, my dad helped her get situated in a new home and helped take the load off so she could focus on her kids. I have to say that my dad lived an upright life.

Jesus told a guy parable that I think fits my dad:

> "There was a man who had two sons. He went to the first and said, 'Son, go and work today in the vineyard.'
>
> " 'I will not,' he answered, but later he changed his mind and went.
>
> "Then the father went to the other son and said the same thing. He answered, 'I will, sir,' but he did not go.
>
> "Which of the two did what his father wanted?" (Matthew 21:28–31).

The point of the parable is this: Talk is cheap. Whether you say you are a Christian or you talk like a Christian or you put on a good Christian face around the other saints at church doesn't matter much. The real test is whether you really do what the Father wants. So, I have concluded that how I think my dad should have lived to gain salvation doesn't matter. What does matter is the question of whether he did what the

Father wants, and I can leave the answer to that question in the Father's hands.

At this point, guys, being guys, usually say, "OK, I'm ready. What can I do?" And the answer is, "Lots of things!"

When my wife, Joyce, and daughter Marisa and I arrived at our first church assignment out of college, we wondered how we were going to unload our moving truck by ourselves. We needn't have worried at all. As the truck driver opened the doors of the moving van, a group of men arrived and started unloading the boxes and furniture. We knew they were from our new church, but we discovered that wasn't the whole story. "We call ourselves the 'Helping Hands,' " one of them told me. "We're a group of retired guys, and we're always looking for someone who needs help."

These guys did handy work for people, ran errands, and generally did anything helpful that they could find to do. Their activities served three purposes: They kept them from becoming bored, they got them out of the house so the men's wives could have some peace, and these activities were the men's spiritual offering to God. Just doing what guys do best brought them a sense of closeness to God. Their spiritual worship to God came in the form of simple acts of kindness for others.

A Father's Day road rally

The men's group in one church I pastored held an annual road rally on Father's Day. They invited fathers and sons from the community to take part. The day began with the road rally itself. The timekeepers sent out the carloads of families from the church parking lot every thirty seconds, with a list of directions to the first checkpoint. The checkpoints were community landmarks; volunteers there gave out directions to the next stop. When everyone had returned from the rally, the men awarded prizes to several teams: the team that came in closest to a prearranged time, the team that ran the course fastest, the team that took the longest time to complete the course, and the team that got farthest off course. (I won a nice gift certificate in this category one year.)

Back at the church, the Pathfinders gave a free carwash to the participants, and local auto buffs brought their classics for a car show. After some refreshments, the men auctioned pies and other goodies as a benefit for local charities like the D.A.R.E. program and a home for battered women and children. It was a great time for guys to get together and bond with their families. It was a way for our Christian guys to do something good for their community. And it was an act of spiritual worship for every man involved.

My friend Fred Ramsey founded a wonderfully practical ministry called Re-Creation Unlimited. One of the services he offers is a community-education course that local churches can provide. Called Women in the Driver's Seat, it is an outreach seminar for women in the community, teaching them how to troubleshoot minor car problems and perform simple repairs safely. They learn how to change a flat tire and check their auto's belts and fluid levels, how to choose a mechanic, and how to negotiate a good deal when selling or buying a car.

Who are the best instructors for this seminar? The guys in the church, of course! The typical backyard mechanic can teach this course as well as a physician can conduct a stop-smoking seminar. It's a perfect way for guys to use their gifts for ministry. It not only provides a service to their community and gives priceless exposure for their church, but the guys who participate also gain a powerful sense of their connection to God. Nothing provides a greater spiritual boost for a guy than does working at something meaningful for his God, his church, and his community.

When I was a youth pastor, I enjoyed working with Maranatha Volunteers International. Whenever I took a youth group to help with a project, I enjoyed seeing how the older men mentored the kids.

One particular young man in my youth group had a history as a problem teen. He was always getting into some kind of trouble, and the people who knew him constantly reminded him that he was a troublemaker. We nearly had to send him home before we even began working on the project. The other adult leaders and I decided to give him a chance to work; we decided to see how he behaved once he had something to keep him busy.

This kid was big, and the project foreman, who knew nothing about him, took one look at him and said, "You! Come with me." We thought maybe we should tell the foreman that this boy was trouble, but we didn't. *He'll find out soon enough,* we thought.

The foreman never found out. He made this boy his right-hand man. The boy tagged along with the foreman and did whatever he needed him to do. The boy held the measuring tape for the foreman; he cut boards for him and generally shadowed him through the whole project. Whenever the foreman gave the boy a task to do, he fully expected him to carry out the assignment responsibly, and to our amazement, he did. We'd never seen him behave so well.

That foreman gave this boy a sense of self-worth that he never had experienced before. All the foreman did was to perform his spiritual act of worship to God by going about his business in a Christlike manner.

Worshiping by cutting firewood

Once when I was talking with a group of men, I asked them what they do that they consider an act of spiritual worship to God. I especially wanted to hear about things that they had never considered an offering to the Lord. One man's eyes lit up. "I cut firewood," he said.

"So what?" came the response from others in the group. A lot of guys cut firewood.

"No," he said, "when I do this, I really feel closer to God than at any other time." Then he explained. This guy cuts some wood for himself, but he cuts a lot more for the elderly members of his church. It seems like an ordinary, natural thing to do, but when he thought about it, he realized this was his time of communion with the Lord.

When he explained what he did for these people and what it meant to him spiritually, several other guys in the group asked if they could help. He wasn't sure at first—he didn't want to lose his private time in the woods with the Lord. Eventually, though, he gave in to the requests from guys who wanted to join him; there were more needy people than he could help. But he set some ground rules: Those who wanted to work with him had to agree to do it as a personal spiritual journey. They must agree to pray before they started and to spend much of their work time in quiet meditation to the Lord.

I learned more about my dad's spiritual life a few years after his death, when my grandmother died. A couple of my dad's brothers and I went to her house to go through her things and settle some family affairs. I'd never spent much time with them, but these events in life tend to get people to open up. Finding some particular knick-knack or keepsake spurs memories that gets people talking.

I discovered that my dad was a PK—a preacher's kid. I hadn't known that before—my grandfather died well before

I was born, and his life never came up in family discussions. That revelation helped me start putting things together in a way that made sense to me.

My grandmother attended the no-musical-instruments-allowed Church of Christ on the north end of town. My mother attended the very musical Church of Christ in the center of town. This may be speculation, but it works for me: I reasoned that Dad felt caught in a no-win situation. I know that neither my mom nor my grandma would pressure Dad to attend her particular church, but he may have decided to stay out of a potential minefield all together. Instead of attending one church or the other, he kept the peace by attending none. His church attendance and spiritual life consisted of helping the widows and orphans. I like to think that this is when he connected with God. That was his spiritual act of worship. I believe that Dad's spirituality, like that of many other guys, was in his doing.

For Personal Reflection

- When do you feel closest to the Lord?

- What is your favorite sanctuary in which to worship the Lord?

- What do you think Jesus would like you to do to develop a closer friendship with Him?

CHAPTER 7

Don't Just Do Some-thing, Be Something!

One challenge guys face is moving from the realm of just doing Christian things to actually being a Spirit-filled Christian guy. For guys, it's helpful to have an idea what exactly it is we are supposed to be. The Lord told the people of Judah and Jerusalem, " 'I said, "Obey me and do everything I command you, and you will be my people, and I will be your God" ' " (Jeremiah 11:4).

So what are we supposed to be? "My people." God's people. Guys can relate to this phrase. We know who our people are. Our people are our families, our co-workers, our neighbors, the guys in the hot-rod club, the locals down at the corner cafe. In other words, they are the people we associate with and those with whom we feel at home. In other words, God said that we are to be guys who can feel comfortable associating with Him.

It's time to revisit our two lists. The first list comes from Galatians 5:19–21. It describes who we are without Christ: "The acts of the sinful nature are obvious: sexual immorality, impurity and debauchery; idolatry and witchcraft; hatred, discord, jealousy, fits of rage, selfish ambition, dissensions, factions and envy; drunkenness, orgies, and the like. I warn you, as I did before, that those who live like this will not inherit the kingdom of God."

If you see yourself in this list, you won't feel comfortable associating with Jesus Christ. If fact, you'll feel downright uncomfortable around Him! You'll want Jesus to just go away and leave you alone. His presence will make you feel ashamed of yourself, and the sense of guilt will be nearly unbearable. Those who want to live this way never even want to hear the name of Jesus, let alone associate with Him or His people.

When Joyce and I became Christians, we found our "friends" disassociating themselves from us. We didn't avoid them, but they sure avoided us. One day soon after our baptism, we spotted the girlfriend of the guitarist in my former rock band out hitchhiking. Of course we'd give her a ride—you never knew what kind of creepy person might try to pick her up, and she'd be safe with us. We pulled over to the curb a few yards ahead of her. She started to run up to our car, but she stopped when she recognized us. Looking in our mirror, we saw this girl wave at us, but she didn't use all the fingers on her hand. Then she abruptly turned and stomped away. Talk about a feeling of rejection! She wouldn't even allow us to do her a favor.

I don't think we were particularly obnoxious or judgmental because of our new faith, but boy, did our old friends feel uncomfortable around us. In their eyes, we were no longer "their people." We were God's people.

The second list, outlined in Galatians 5:22, 23, describes those who can feel at home in God's presence. This is who we are with Christ: "The fruit of the Spirit is love, joy, peace, patience, kindness, goodness, faithfulness, gentleness and self-control. Against such things there is no law." When this list describes you, you'll feel right at home with God. You'll be "His people."

Getting the Spirit

The next guy question that arises is, "So, how do I get the Holy Spirit in my life?" We want to know the practical steps to make this happen. We want the map. We want the manual. Even if we don't read the instructions before we put the new patio table together, we like to have it for reference!

Again, Jesus—a guy—gives us a great guy passage that we can relate to. Luke 11:9–13 tells us how to have the Holy Spirit in our lives: " 'Which of you fathers, if your son asks for a fish, will give him a snake instead? Or if he asks for an egg will give him a scorpion? If you then, though you are evil, know how to give good gifts to your children, how much more will your Father in heaven give the Holy Spirit to those who ask Him!' "

Any passage of Scripture that includes snakes and scorpions along with the Holy Spirit is a real guy's text! Jesus actually tells a joke here. If your son asked you for a fish, would you give him a snake instead? "Well," I think, "only if he didn't see me put it on his plate!" Then he'd scream until he saw that it was really just a rubber snake, and we'd have a good laugh and think about how we could pull that one on his mom. Eventually, good sense would return (that's another gift of the Holy Spirit), and we'd realize that we don't want to sleep in the tool shed for the next month, so we'd put the snake in the toy box. Then my boy and I would go fishing.

Jesus' point is that we parents really do enjoy giving our kids gifts. Maybe too much—the cover story on the *Newsweek* magazine sitting on the table in my tent-trailer as I write these words is "How to Say 'No' to Your Kids—Setting Limits in an Age of Excess." Apparently, we can give our kids too many toys.

One year, my daughter wanted a snowboard for her birthday. Of course, I went right out and bought her a snowboard.

Then came the dilemma: "How am I going to wrap this thing?" I'm a guy, remember? My wrapping jobs look like the final result after the kids sneak their gifts from under the Christmas tree, unwrap them to see what they are, and then slap the paper and tape back on to hide what they did. (Now you know how I learned to wrap gifts!)

I thought about just covering the board with a couple of rolls of duct tape, but I reconsidered. Then the brainstorm hit. On her birthday, I put the board on the backseat of my Trooper, in the spot where my daughter usually sat. Then I went in the house and said, "Marisa, you left a big mess in my car. I want you to go out and clean all of your garbage out of my backseat *now!*" (OK, so that wasn't true, but this was for a good cause, and I figured I could ask for forgiveness later.)

Boy was she mad! She knew she hadn't made a mess, and she was going to prove it. Joyce and I just sat on the couch and watched out the living-room window as her anger turned to joy when she opened the Trooper door. Yes, we love giving gifts to our kids.

Jesus gave us this picture of the joy that we dads have when we give stuff to our kids, then He said, "That's the way your heavenly Father feels when you ask for the Holy Spirit!" (Except for the part about really giving the snake to your son. I made that up.)

Just ask

The hard part for guys is asking for anything. We're self-sufficient, remember? It's a blow to our self-image to be dependent on anyone for anything. Asking for help goes against our natural "guy-hood."

Remember when you really wanted that lever-action Winchester 30-30 for Christmas? You wanted to ask your dad for it because he's a guy and he'd understand, but you knew that

Mom and Dad were having a hard time making ends meet this year and Christmas might be a bit skimpy. But you put it on your Christmas list anyway, in little letters so it wouldn't seem like you really wanted it but with a star by it so they couldn't miss it. Hey, it never hurts to ask. Guys may not like it when others speak to us in riddles, but we don't mind dropping a few hints of our own!

Think about the joy you felt when you opened the box and saw the smooth, brown stock and freshly oiled barrel. Now that you're a parent, you can probably imagine the joy your mom and dad felt as they watched you open it. They had sacrificed to provide that gift, but they felt good making that sacrifice for your happiness.

Your heavenly Father sacrificed to provide your salvation. And He knows what Jesus went through to give you the opportunity to have His Spirit in your heart. Imagine the joy He feels when His love and joy and peace fill you. He wants you to be rid of the first list and be completely immersed in the second.

You want the Holy Spirit? Here's your assignment—your to-do list for today: Just ask. God is happy to answer this prayer because He wants to do whatever it takes to include you among His people.

For Personal Reflection

- What is the best gift you've ever received?
- What is the best gift you've ever given?
- When other people look at you, what do you want them to see?

CHAPTER 8

High-Octane Spiritual Fuel

A few years ago, I was fixing up a 1970 Opel GT. It ran, but not very well. If you ever plan to fix up a 1970 Opel GT, understand this: Parts are very rare (some are nonexistent), repair manuals are out of print, and few mechanics know a thing about them. So I was having a real challenge getting the thing to run right.

One day when I was working on it, it started coughing and sputtering and eventually died. I tried to restart it, but it coughed, sputtered, and died again. I tinkered with the engine and adjusted some things, but it just kept getting worse until it wouldn't even fire. So I asked myself, "What would Joyce suggest I check?"

You have to know something about Joyce. She knows little about mechanics, but I've learned to listen to her suggestions. Once when I was trying to fix a car, she asked, "Have you checked the fuel pump?"

Of course, I hadn't checked the fuel pump. It couldn't be the fuel pump. It had to be the carburetor. (It wasn't.) Or the exhaust manifold. (It wasn't.) Or the catalytic converter. (It wasn't.) Many hours, much effort, and hundreds of dollars later, I discovered that it *was* the fuel pump!

So I wondered what Joyce would suggest. She would probably ask, "Does it have gas in it?"

Of course, it has gas in it. But I decided that before she had the chance to come see me struggling and ask the question, I'd check just to make sure. I disconnected the fuel line, switched on the fuel pump—and got about a pint of foul, junky fuel. I put in a couple gallons of high-octane fuel, and it fired right up.

The first principle

Does your spiritual life ever seem to cough and sputter as though it's not hitting on all eight cylinders? Does it ever seem to be dying? The first principle of having a smooth-running spiritual life is this: You must have fuel in your tank.

One night, my friend Dan and I went to a party in a field along Teeters Creek, by Dorena Lake. You had to really want to party to go to a party at Teeters Creek because you have to drive through the creek to get there. No problem. Dan had a '62 Jeep CJ2A. We crawled all over the hills around Cottage Grove, Oregon, in that thing, so crossing Teeters Creek was no problem.

I'm sure we enjoyed the party. I don't remember much, except that later that night we decided to go four-wheeling. Five of us piled into the Jeep, and up the hill we went. It was great, except for one thing: Dan's old Jeep didn't have a working fuel gauge. His fuel gauge was a stick that he poked down into the gas tank. Dan hadn't checked the gas for a couple of days, and sure enough, up on top of the hill we ran out of gas.

No problem. We were up the hill, and there were five of us, so we could push the thing back down to the party and borrow some gas to get home. And we did pretty well as long as we were headed downhill. But when we came to a few places where the road went uphill, it was hard. Our strength was great on the downhill sections of road. Our strength was OK on the flat sections. But when we came to even a slight uphill climb, we had to get a run at it—sometimes two or three runs at it—and push with all our might to get over the hump. We finally made it back to the party, but we were physically shot. I don't recommend moving a car using your own strength as fuel. Gasoline works much better.

That's true of our spiritual lives as well. I learned that firsthand.

Every year at the camp meeting run by the Oregon Conference of Seventh-day Adventists, I spend the last Sunday directing traffic at the Adventist Book Center Sunday sale. It can be a real mess there. There's limited parking, lots of campers show up with their motor homes and big travel trailers, and the street outside the bookstore parking lot is busy with fast-moving traffic.

We have, however, a very organized plan for moving the traffic through. The plan specifies that the north driveway is designated "Entrance Only" during the sale. In order to leave, you have to circle around the building that houses the conference offices and exit at the south driveway. The problem is that during the rest of the year, the north driveway serves as both an entrance and an exit, and some people who are used to exiting at the north driveway consider it a hassle to have to go to the south gate. But it's the only way to keep the traffic moving safely off that dangerous street.

As I was directing traffic a couple of years ago, someone started to turn toward the north driveway. I pointed him toward the lower lot so he could go around and exit safely. Instead of turning around, however, he started driving toward me. I pointed to the "One Way" sign, but he kept coming.

A big motor home was trying to enter the driveway, and a line of traffic was forming behind it. I needed to get this guy out of the way so we could get the traffic off the street, but he wouldn't budge. So I told him, "Sir, you have to turn around and go around the building, or we could have an accident." At that, he gunned his engine and careened right toward me. When he did so, I jumped out of the way and yelled, "You're gonna kill someone, you ____!"—and out of my mouth came a word I hadn't said in more than sixteen years.

I couldn't believe I'd said that word (even though I still think it was an accurate description of the guy). Then I glanced to my right and saw a man looking at me. I don't know if he saw the whole incident. That doesn't matter. All I know is that he heard me yell a word that he'd probably never heard a church leader utter before. That's when it hit me: My tank was empty. I was spiritually unprepared for any challenges that day. During that camp meeting week, I'd been running around doing the Lord's work: I'd been rushing to meet deadlines, and I'd been dealing with problems. But while I'd been steadily emptying my spiritual fuel tank, I hadn't been taking time to refill it. Everything went well as long I didn't have to push through any problems. But when a little issue came up, I had no fuel left to deal with it. I responded with my human nature—rage—not with the fruits of the Spirit—patience, peace, and love.

I wonder now, what if that bystander was a seeker, still trying to discover what God and Jesus and Christianity are all about? God had the opportunity to show that man how a Spirit-filled Christian handles conflict. But because my spiritual fuel tank was dry, the man got an exhibition of the crud in my heart. Instead of seeing God at work, he saw the ugliness that still rages within me when the Holy Spirit isn't there to kill it. I don't care what that guy thinks of me, but I do care what he thinks about my God and His church.

When you have those moments when you do or say something that you wish you could erase, check your spiritual fuel tank. Is it dry? In my mind there's nothing more dangerous than a person who claims to be a Christian—especially a Seventh-day Adventist Christian—who is running on fumes. When people of the world see supposed Christians running on empty, they say, "If that's what a Christian is like, I'll pass." Don't ever let it happen to you. Keep your tank full so you can deal with multiple challenges without running dry.

The second principle

The second principle of having a smooth-running spiritual life is this: You must have the right fuel in your tank.

Dennis was the keyboard player in my rock band when we were in high school. He bought an old Ford for fifty dollars when we were juniors. We'd use it to cruise around the school and hit the fast-food joints during lunch break.

One day we were cruising a few blocks away from the school when we discovered (can you guess?) that the fuel gauge didn't work. Even though it read three-quarters of a tank, we ran out of gas. We should have guessed there was a problem when the gauge gave the same reading for two weeks, but we just thought the car was getting great gas mileage!

We had to get back to school because Dennis was already on academic probation for skipping class, and there was no way the two of us were going to push that big old boat anywhere. But Dennis came up with a solution. He'd been painting his mom's house, and he still had a can of turpentine in his trunk.

Did you know that an old Ford will run on turpentine? Yes, it will.

Do you know how far an old Ford will run on turpentine? In our case, about four blocks—from the corner of Sixth Street and Johnson Avenue to Tenth Street and Taylor Avenue, where the high school was, and that's it. I'm sure the valves were like crispy French fries by then. After the tow truck hauled the old beater off for scrap, we never saw it again. Fortunately, Dennis was out only the fifty bucks he'd paid for the car plus whatever it cost to have it towed off.

Just as turpentine is the wrong fuel to put into your gas tank, so the Bible warns us not to try to run our spiritual life on the wrong "fuel." Ezekiel 13:3 says, " 'This is what the Sovereign LORD says: Woe to the foolish prophets who follow their own spirit and have seen nothing!' " There are people who give all kinds of strong opinions about things, but they're not from God. They haven't seen a thing. First John 4:1, 2 says it this way: "Dear friends, do not believe every spirit, but test the spirits to see whether they are from God, because many false prophets have gone out into the world. This is how you can recognize the Spirit of God: Every spirit that acknowledges that Jesus Christ has come in the flesh is from God."

I've heard from some very spiritual people that Jesus was a good man, that He was a great teacher, that He was an enlightened prophet. These people have a spiritual life. But this is how you can tell if they have God's true Spirit: They will acknowledge Jesus Christ. When people have the Holy Spirit in their life, other people will know it. It won't be a secret. Those people will publicly proclaim Jesus Christ.

What does that mean? Look at the name: *Jesus* is the Greek form of the Hebrew name *Joshua,* which means "the Lord saves." The angel Gabriel told Joseph to name the boy *Jesus* because " 'he will save his people from their sins' " (Matthew 1:21). *Christ* is the Greek form of the Hebrew title *Messiah,* which means "the anointed one." The Messiah is the Lord, the Ruler of your life. To acknowledge Jesus Christ is to say, "I can't save myself. I need a Savior, and I will do His will for the rest of my life." People who have God's Spirit will publicly proclaim, "There is no other name under heaven given to men by which we may be saved" (Acts 4:12).

The passage in 1 John goes one step further. It says that people who have the Spirit that comes from God will acknowledge "that Jesus Christ has come in the flesh." In other words, they will acknowledge that our Creator God stepped down from heaven and died for our sins. If that's what they say, then their spirit is from God.

Speaking of false prophets, Jesus said, " 'By their fruit you will recognize them' " (Matthew 7:16). If you want to know what spirit is leading a person, often all you have to do is to stand back and watch for a while. I've seen several people who appear to be very godly turn out to be charlatans. And on the other hand, as I've watched some simple, humble men over time, I've been surprised to see them reveal a depth of godly wisdom.

The wrong spiritual fuel looks like the first of the two lists we studied earlier: "The acts of the sinful nature are obvious: sexual immorality, impurity and debauchery; idolatry and witchcraft; hatred, discord, jealousy, fits of rage, selfish ambition, dissensions, factions and envy; drunkenness, orgies, and the like. I warn you, as I did before, that those who live like this will not inherit the kingdom of God" (Galatians 5:19–21). This is a danger for men. We are task-oriented, and this list is based on our acts, our deeds.

The right, high-octane spiritual fuel has the ingredients of the second list: "The fruit of the Spirit is love, joy, peace, patience, kindness, goodness, faithfulness, gentleness and self-control. Against such things there is no law" (Galatians

5:22, 23). This list is not based on our deeds. Rather, it describes who we are—Spirit-filled Christians who look like Jesus.

Make sure you are filled with the right spiritual fuel.

To review: In order to have a smooth-running spiritual life, you must have fuel in your tank, and it must be the right fuel.

Let's be guys who live the life Paul described in Romans 8:9–11: "You, however, are controlled not by the sinful nature but by the Spirit, if the Spirit of God lives in you. And if anyone does not have the Spirit of Christ, he does not belong to Christ. But if Christ is in you, your body is dead because of sin, yet your spirit is alive because of righteousness. And if the Spirit of him who raised Jesus from the dead is living in you, he who raised Christ from the dead will also give life to your mortal bodies through his Spirit, who lives in you."

When you are filled with God's Holy Spirit, you can live a truly high-octane Christian life.

For Personal Reflection

- Can you think of a time when you were spiritually dry? Why was your spiritual tank empty?

- What fills your spiritual tank? What makes you feel the most spiritually alive?

- If you noticed that your best friend appeared spiritually drained, what would you do to help?

CHAPTER 9

Scrubbing Down
Your Workplace

It was a worship service any guy would love. It was Easter weekend, and the theme for the day was "Crossing the Gulf." In the center aisle of the sanctuary, directly in front of the platform, we had placed the beginnings of a ramp. The ramp led up toward the platform, but it wasn't complete. We had left a four-foot gap between the ramp and the stage.

I preached on the gulf that exists between God and us because of sin, and then I told how Jesus bridged that gap by His death on the cross. While I was speaking, two deacons came forward and built the remainder of the ramp. By the time I finished the sermon, they had built a fully functional bridge from the center aisle to the platform. This was a real guy's worship service—we got to build something!

After the bridge was complete, I invited the congregation to come forward, symbolically crossing the bridge from death to life. Several young people were on the platform to give each person a Popsicle-stick cross the kids had made and a booklet explaining the plan of salvation.

The thought that Jesus gave His life to build the bridge to heaven for us moved the congregation. Some came forward with tears in their eyes. As I watched the people come, I noticed a man and a woman I'd never seen before. Though the woman looked much older than the man, he leaned on her for support. They received their gifts and returned to their seats. I thought nothing more about them until the phone rang two weeks later. Wally, one of my deacons, was calling.

"Pastor Chuck," Wally began, "would you go with me sometime to visit a fella?"

"Sure, Wally," I replied. "What's up?"

"Well, you know that service you did a couple of weeks ago?" he said. "A guy named Keith attended. He was there with his former mother-in-law. I think that's the only time he's ever been to church."

My mind flashed to the man and the older woman. "Yeah, I remember them."

"Keith called me that afternoon," Wally continued. "He wanted me to come over and talk to him about God sometime, and, well, I think we should do it soon. He's real sick."

I met Wally at the home Keith shared with his former mother-in-law. When we saw Keith, he could barely lift his head. Cancer. Keith told us that he gave his heart to the Lord as he walked across that makeshift bridge at church. We prayed with him and left, promising to return for more visits. We never got the chance. Keith died two days later.

I asked Wally about Keith's background and how long they'd known each other. "That's the thing," Wally said. "I don't really know him. We worked on a job together over twenty years ago. I was driving a truck, and he worked on a road crew. When he called the other day, he said, 'I knew that if I ever wanted to talk about God, I wanted to talk to you.' I'm as surprised as anyone."

What brought Keith to church on that particular Sabbath? I believe it was the Holy Spirit. What inspired Keith to call

Wally? I believe it was the Holy Spirit, who had used Wally in the workplace more than twenty years earlier.

Guys love challenges, and Jesus has given us a challenge. He said, " 'You are the salt of the earth' " (Matthew 5:13).

One of the things that salt does is to season whatever environment it's placed in. It influences how we taste things. (Try eating French fries without salt!) Wally didn't give Keith a twenty-eight-part Bible study, but whatever he did or said on that road job made an impression on Keith that he remembered decades later. It was probably some little act of kindness. An average guy may make little impact on this world, but a Spirit-filled average guy can influence someone for eternity.

Workplace dangers

While faithful Christian guys can make a positive impact on their workplace, it can be cruel to them. Often, other guys ridicule Christians. They consider Christianity to be something that restricts their fun, and they think anyone foolish enough to follow Christ loses the good things of life. Some see Christianity as a crutch for guys who aren't manly enough to take care of their own problems—if you need Christ, you must be weak. Some are under conviction themselves, and the only way they can justify their course in life and silence the still, small Voice pulling at their heart is to ridicule Christ's followers.

Sometimes Christian guys feel pushed to violate their principles. The temptation can be something as simple as being asked to falsify on an invoice the amount of work done. Or it can be something huge, like being told they must work on Sabbath or lose their job. It's hard to stand for Christ when your job is on the line. Some guys regularly face unemployment because they stand for Christian principles.

Also, the environment in the break room is often unpleasant. Guys are exposed to language they're trying to forget, jokes that are no longer funny, pin-ups on the wall that tempt them to violate the seventh commandment, and even something as common, and yet insidious, as cigarette smoke.

I quit smoking a dozen times before I became a Christian. My stop-smoking resolution was an annual New Year's Eve event. I usually made it three days. Once, though, I quit for one whole year, and I knew I had it licked—until I went to work at the boxcar repair shop. I was only there a few weeks when I started having urges again. I resisted the urges for a while, but they became unbearable. (I wasn't a Christian yet and didn't have God's strength to rely on.) Finally, I told myself, "OK, I'll just smoke one cigarette; then the urge will be gone and that's it."

That was dumb! I was back to smoking a pack a day by the end of the week. When I realized I'd been blindsided by the habit again, I wanted to find the culprit that had hijacked me, so I mentally reviewed what had happened. Then I realized that every day, three times a day, a fog of secondhand smoke blanketed me in the break room. I had picked up the smoking habit again well before I ever lit up a cigarette.

What is a Christian guy to do? Be salt. Before the days of refrigeration, people rubbed salt on meat to prevent the growth of bacteria. Salt kept the meat pure, unspoiled. Salt seasons its environment, and it purifies it.

Before I became a Christian, I spent some time working for a plumber who subcontracted for several builders in the area. One morning we pulled up at a work site of a contractor I hadn't seen before. As we did so, my boss gave us this warning: "Watch your language while you're here, and don't tell dirty jokes. This guy is a Christian."

I didn't know how we'd survive the day. No cussing? No bad jokes? I had to behave!

You know what? We made it just fine.

However, the point is that the boss didn't give us the order because the contractor, Vernon Johnson, was a grouch about his Christianity. If someone slipped and let out a four-letter description of how it felt to smash his thumb with a hammer, Vernon wouldn't give us a lecture about foul language. No, we watched our mouths because we knew he was a nice man and we didn't want to offend him. He did high-quality work, and he treated workers with kindness and respect. So those who worked around him returned that respect, and for a few days, our mouths were purified.

By treating our co-workers as Christ would, we Christian guys can earn the respect of others and have a purifying influence on our environment. I actually learned to appreciate the times we plumbed Vernon Johnson's homes. It just felt good to be in a clean atmosphere.

Later, when I began attending the local Seventh-day Adventist church, I got to know Vernon better. He was a deacon there, a Spirit-filled, Seventh-day Adventist deacon guy who earned the respect of other guys in the community. Imagine that—we really can be salt!

Dave, the trucker

Another guy who has seasoned and purified his environment is Dave, a truck driver. He rubs shoulders with all kinds of other guys, and he knows how to take their comments about his faith.

One fellow trucker was usually cool to religion. Every now and then he'd make a comment to Dave about his faith, and often it wasn't complimentary. Dave would just let the comment go and semi-jokingly reply, "Well, I'll still pray for you anyway!"

The man kept up his tough demeanor around the other truckers, but one day he became very serious when no one else was around. He told Dave that his son had died, and then he looked Dave in the eye and asked him, "Where is he?"

Dave didn't give a detailed Bible study on the state of man at death, but he did assure his friend of God's love and care in his time of need. He helped the man understand that God is in control of the situation, and guys can pour out their heart to Him at any time. Because Dave always returned the man's cutting comments with kindness and a bit of humor, this hardhearted truck driver knew he could go to Dave with his spiritual need.

This truck driver had two methods of dealing with his son's death—drinking and drugs. One day he looked particularly depressed, so Dave said, "You know, when the drink and the drugs don't do it for you anymore, Jesus can give you the help you need." Because Dave had never bashed the man with religion, he listened to Dave and pondered his words. Not too long after that, the man confided to Dave that he'd given his heart to Jesus. Today, Dave says, "He's probably a better Christian than I am!" Guys in the workplace can reach people that we preachers will never touch.

Dave would often roll down his window and visit with the flaggers while he waited for the pilot car to come and guide him through the construction site. One day a flagger stopped Dave. He had spoken with this girl at other sites, and they were comfortable enough to tease each other. This day, however, she wasn't in a joking mood. With a tone of sadness in her voice, she asked Dave, "What do you think about abortion?"

Dave didn't jump right in with an answer. Instead, he decided to explore the question a bit further before giving his thoughts. "Why do you ask?" he probed.

The flagger knew that Dave was a Christian, and she felt he was safe to talk to. "I'm pregnant," she replied.

As they talked there along the road, Dave in his truck and the girl holding the stop sign, he discovered that she wasn't married and her boyfriend wanted her to abort the pregnancy. Her real question wasn't "What do you think about abortion?" It was "Should I get an abortion?"

Because of their comfortable friendship, she let Dave give her some fatherly guidance. He didn't preach, and he didn't lecture. He was simply there for her in her time of need.

Here's what Dave says about how to be a Christian guy in the workplace: Our Seventh-day Adventist Christian doctrines are great, but we need to meet people in their real-life situations. The best way to practice our spirituality in the workplace is simply to be a safe person to talk to, because someday our co-workers will need someone to talk to about their spiritual issues. You can be that person.

So, be salt. Season and purify your workplace environment.

For Personal Reflection

- Rate the spiritual environment at your workplace on a scale of 1 (hell on earth) to 5 (it's better than church).

- What influences in your workplace threaten your spiritual life?

- What can you do to season and purify your workplace?

CHAPTER 10

Are You Sure SDA Isn't Spelled SAD?

Early in my ministry, one of the members of my first church invited Joyce and me to his gun club for some target practice. I think he assumed two things—first, that since I'm a pastor, I would have no clue which end of the gun to hold, and second, since I'm a pastor, I'd probably say no since Christians (and especially pastors) aren't supposed to have fun.

Joyce and I blew his second assumption by saying yes. Sure, Joyce and I hadn't touched a gun in the past six years, but it sounded like fun. And, yes, I believe that Christians can have fun, and there are even some "guy" things that are both fun and spiritually acceptable.

When Joyce and I arrived at the club, our friend told us we would be shooting silhouettes. My blank stare probably reaffirmed his first assumption. I'd never heard of such a thing. My target-shooting experience consisted of plinking cans and bottles and shooting clay pigeons and the occasional bull's-eye target tacked to a bale of hay. I always shot standing and holding the rifle stock snug against my shoulder or sitting and resting the gun on some solid object.

That's not how you shoot silhouettes. So, I had to learn a new style of shooting.

To shoot silhouettes, you lie on your back, pull your knees up, and rest a long-barreled .22-caliber pistol against your leg above your ankle. Then you shoot at a metal target, a silhouette of a coyote.

Sure enough, my first shot went high, churning up a puff of dirt above the silhouette. My friend chuckled a bit, sure that his first assumption was the only thing on target this day.

I calculated how high above the target I had shot at this particular distance, adjusted my aim accordingly, and *ping!* I hit the "coyote's" head.

"This is cool!" I yelled as I pinged another slug off the target. *Ping! Ping! Ping!* I emptied the revolver into the target.

"Joyce, you have to try this!" I said, laughing as I reloaded the pistol. I showed her how to sight the gun on the target, and she pinged away.

After our friend got over his initial amazement at our shooting prowess, we confessed that we grew up around guns and had done some trap shooting and the more traditional target shooting. This was, however, our first attempt at silhouettes.

It was a fun, harmless way to spend a Sunday morning blowing off some steam. My church-member friend also gained some new insight into Christian life: It's OK for Christians, even pastors, to have fun. And that fun can include some traditionally "guy" things.

We often feel that anything fun must be against our Christian faith, and we end up compartmentalizing our lives into that which is good and spiritual (church activities) and that which we really enjoy (if it's fun, it must be bad). In this compartmentalization, we mentally balance the good against the bad. In other words, if we do something fun, we must then do some churchy-type activity to make up for it. We figure that if we endure enough "spiritual" activities, then we can go out and have some fun. It's kind of a modern form of the sale of indulgences.

I maintain that there are many ways to have fun that are entirely compatible with our Christianity. Even Jesus had fun. He enjoyed social functions. Why did He hang out with Mary, Martha, and Lazarus? They were fun to be around. There is a place in the guy's Christian life for hobbies and enjoyable interests.

You can use your own hobbies and interests, things that are fun, for the glory of God. A great way to bring a sense of spirituality into your hobbies is to use them as mentoring events. Do you belong to a gun club? Find some young people who lack positive role models, and teach them how to shoot in a safe, responsible way. There's something about hitting a bull's-eye on a paper target that inspires kids to aim for proper goals in life—if someone they respect takes the time to help them focus their sights.

When I spoke on this topic for a men's group, one man made a confession: He enjoyed hunting. Of course, no one was shocked or offended; they all knew he enjoyed hunting. He felt there was something un-Christian about it, however, because he was a vegetarian and didn't eat the meat. Despite that, every year he bought tags, loaded up his belt with ammo, and went out and bagged a deer and an elk. Then he butchered the animals, wrapped up the meat, and took it to a local food bank. He enjoyed his hobby and helped feed the hungry at the same time. Jesus said something about this in Matthew 25:31–46. Look it up!

You should have seen the lights go on in the eyes of the other guys in the room when they heard this. *What a great idea!* they thought. Before the day was through, several of them were planning their next hunting trips together. One guy's passion became an opportunity for other guys to get together, have fun, and help someone else at the same time.

Shooting big game and small

If you are creative, you can come up with enjoyable modifications of hobbies you no longer participate in. I don't hunt anymore, but my buddy Leon came up with a great substitute. He is handy in a woodshop, so he constructed gunstocks for our cameras, complete with triggers. I bought a huge, 500 mm lens, and when I attach it to my camera and mount the whole outfit on the stock, the result looks like a massive big-game rifle. The feeling of power when you lock onto a huge buck and click away is awesome, and I think the deer really appreciate it too!

You can even make a few dollars at it. I had a photo of a four-point mule deer (in velvet) published on the cover of a magazine. A couple of hunters watched Leon and I shooting some bucks in a wildlife refuge and thought it was such a great idea that they ordered some prints from Leon. He made enough to pay for the photo trip.

We've shot deer, elk, antelope, mink, ducks, geese, hawks, and eagles. Some of the animals we shoot are on the endangered species list, but we've never broken any laws by bagging their pictures. We never have to buy a license or a tag, and with digital cameras, we never worry about ammo (film). Any season is hunting season when you shoot your game with a camera. And I don't have to be the "dog" anymore! Christian guys can have fun and be spiritual servants of God simultaneously.

You'll love this next idea. In fact, by the time you finish this chapter, you'll be able to say to your wife, "Honey, I need a new, big-screen TV," and you'll have a convincing argument that she'll surely agree with.

One of my pastor friends has a big-screen TV. Every football season he invites all the neighborhood guys over to watch Monday Night Football. They get together, watch the game, and eat snacks—a real social extravaganza for guys. During halftime, this pastor mutes the sound and the guys talk. Did you get that? Guys talk! They talk about how things went at work last week, how the kids are doing at school, and sometimes they even pray about whatever life-events are challenging them. Then they watch the second half.

I think the key to this sharing time is that they know it isn't open-ended. Halftime doesn't last very long, so their fear of endless soul searching is relieved. But the conversation does bring the guys closer together as friends and neighbors as well as open their hearts to God.

Here's the formula:

Big-screen TV
+ Monday Night Football
+ guys and snacks
= an evening of wholesome, spiritual fun

And you can tell your wife I said so!

Another pastor got a group of guys together to watch World War II movies. Each week they watched a movie and discussed the historical implications of the event portrayed. That opened the door for the guys to get better acquainted with each other. And when this pastor holds an evangelistic series, his movie buddies are willing to come and hear God's Word. It's fun, it's a guy thing, and it can bring glory to God.

Do you enjoy auto mechanics? Offer to teach your skills to your local Pathfinder club. Who else is teaching today's young people basic auto-care techniques, such as how to change a tire, how to check the oil and radiator coolant, and how to read a repair quote and bill to avoid rip-offs? You'll be raising the next generation of guys and having fun with your hobby at the same time.

Do you ride dirt bikes, quads, or snowmobiles? Talk to the social committee at your church. Maybe there are guys who would like to get together with a group of other guys who don't swear, drink, or hit their wives.

Do you own a boat? Your youth leaders would love an invitation to take their kids out to the lake on a ski day.

OK, I can hear it now: "Honey, I need a _____ [boat, bike, quad, big-screen TV—you fill in the blank!]—Pastor Chuck said so!" I didn't say you could mortgage your family up to your eyeballs to buy a few toys. Live within your means; don't take food off your table or neglect your other responsibilities to enjoy your guy interests. But if you do get a couple of quads, give me a call. I'd love to go sling some mud with you!

Often, guys simply need permission to think of these things as part of their spiritual life. The key is to make sure that your interests aren't inherently immoral. Participate in them as someone full of the fruit of the Spirit, and dedicate your hobbies to the glory of God. He wants you to enjoy life to the fullest, even if you are just a regular guy.

For Personal Reflection

- If Jesus invited you over for a game night, what games would He bring out to play?

- Is your spiritual life fun?

- If it is, then why? If not, then why not?

CHAPTER 11

Because I'm the Dad/ Husband Guy, That's Why

The headline grabbed my attention like a blitzing linebacker locked onto a quarterback in the backfield: "Want a successful marriage? Just do what your wife says."

Seriously.

The article said, "Husbands who give in to their mate's complaints last longer, study finds." Now that sounded ominous. Just what do they mean, "last longer"? Are some wives just waiting for the right opportunity to drop a bit of arsenic in their guy's soda pop if he doesn't comply with their wishes? Could be, but I don't want to even go there! The article reported that the marriages in the study that lasted longest and enjoyed the most happiness were those in which the husband just let things go with a simple, "Yes, dear."

A few days later, Scott Gibson, a physician in my church and also a guy, had this response published in the paper: "A recent study by some psychologists, the same people who brought you electroshock therapy, has shown that the most successful marriages are the ones where—are you ready for the news?—the husband gives in to the wife. As a man who has been married for 15 going on 60 years, I can only say, Well, duh."

Guys have known this all along; apparently these psychologists are not guys. But just because it works this way doesn't make it right.

Sadly, I often see the other side of the coin: guys who need to dominate their wives and kids to feel validated in their so-called manhood. Here's my take on guys who exhibit that behavior: Any man who needs to abuse another person mentally, verbally, physically, or sexually to feel good about himself is one sick puppy and needs help. If you are in that category, stop it! Go get help. That's not what God's guys are all about. The good news is that God offers help and rebirth to even the worst of sinners. With God's help, an abuser can get a fresh start toward healthy relationships and eternal life in His kingdom.

In God's house, no one dominates another, and no one is a doormat. That's the kind of spiritual home we can have right now. Let's agree to be the best family men that we can be with God's help. To start, let's take a look at the biblical guidelines for a happy spiritual family life for guys.

The best counsel on family life that I've found is recorded in two passages of Scripture. Colossians 3:18–21 says, "Wives, submit to your husbands, as is fitting in the Lord. [I would say that I like that verse best of all, but then my wife would smack me upside the head and remind me to read on. I would say, "Yes, dear."] Husbands, love your wives and do not be harsh with them. [OK, this one is good too.] Children, obey your parents in everything, for this pleases the Lord. [Joyce and I both like this one!] Fathers, do not embitter your children or they will become discouraged. [Hey, what about mothers?]" The second passage, Ephesians 5:22–6:4, simply takes these same concepts and expands them. You should prayerfully read it sometime.

The thing I like best about these passages is that they contain something for everyone. No one—not guys, guys' gals, nor guys' kids—is left out. These passages don't set anyone up to dominate anyone else in the family. But since I am speaking to guys here, let me ask two questions: How well do you love your wife? And do you ever embitter your kids?

A TV commercial I saw some time back really caught my attention. It was probably a beer commercial during a football game, but I don't remember what it was selling. The commercial pictured a group of guys watching a game together. While they're watching, one of them gets a phone call from his honey. She ends her part of the conversation by saying, "I love you."

Realizing that all his manly buddies can hear his every word, he responds, "I do too."

"You do what?" she asks.

"I, uh, you know. What you said."

Needless to say, the conversation and the relationship both go downhill from there—and we're reminded again that guys have a hard time expressing their feelings.

If you have that problem, put this book down right now and go and tell your wife and kids how much you love them. They will be speechless the rest of the day, and later on you can watch the game with the guys unhindered. We can do this, guys. Think of this as a challenge—a dare from the Lord: "Husbands, love your wives and do not be harsh with them." We are doers, and love is something you do. We can conquer this goal.

Show it

I asked a group of guys, "What do you do to show your wife how much you love her?" After a few uncomfortable moments of blank stares, one guy spoke up. "I take her to the races with me." Good. That's a start. Apparently, she really enjoys the races, and it's together-time for them. In this case, it's a good thing to do.

One guy sheepishly admitted that he brought home flowers for his wife every now and then. "I had to deal with a couple of problems when I started this, though," he said. "First, she wondered what terrible thing I did that I was trying to cover up. Second, I had to get over the idea that these flowers would wilt in a few days and all that money would be wasted. I finally realized that it is money well spent."

Another guy said, "I make sure I tell her 'I love you' before I leave in the morning. I'm a logger, and if something happens to me in the woods, I want those to be the last words she heard from me." Several of the guys in the group said, "That's good. Way to go, man!"

I read a study once that said that men who kiss their wives before they leave the house live an average of five years longer than those who don't. I think they run into fewer skillets. The logger had never read that study, but he figured it out on his own.

These responses came from typically rugged guys. Some of the other guys at this meeting had to admit they couldn't think of any way that they show their love to their families. Our goal is to have a healthy partnership with our life's mate—maybe even see her as one of the guys. (OK, maybe not!) But if you do your part—love her and be gentle and considerate—and she does her part—submitting to your leadership in the home—you can have a happy, healthy home life that gives glory to God. We can do this. We are guys! Think of it as a challenge from the Lord, a goal that we can conquer.

What kind of dad are you?

Parenting is another animal altogether. Many guys I know didn't have very good parenting skills modeled to them, so they make up their mode of parenting as they go. The Bible's counsel is simply, "Fathers, do not embitter your children or they will become discouraged."

A survey of four different parenting styles revealed three types of parenting that can produce embittered children and one that helps avoid that problem.* The four styles are *authoritarian parenting, uninvolved parenting, indulgent parenting*, and *authoritative parenting*. They are defined this way:

- "Authoritarian parents are highly demanding and directive, but not responsive" to their children's emotional needs.
- "Uninvolved parents are low in both responsiveness and demandingness." In other words, they neglect their kids.
- "Indulgent parents are more responsive than they are demanding. They are nontraditional and lenient, do not require mature behavior, allow considerable self-regulation, and avoid confrontation."
- "Authoritative parents are both demanding and responsive. They monitor and impart clear standards for their children's conduct. Their disciplinary methods are supportive, rather than punitive."

Can you guess which three types you want to avoid, and which one you should practice? The report goes on to say, "Authoritative parenting, which balances clear, high parental demands with emotional responsiveness and recognition of child autonomy, is one of the most consistent family predictors of competence from early childhood through adolescence."†

In other words, give your kids good directions in life, be a mentor to them, and love them unconditionally, and you will have done your best. Guys, we can do this.

"Quality time"

I used to struggle with the notion of "quality time." We live in a very high-pressure society, and the expectation to produce on the job can limit the amount of time dads have with their kids. The notion of "quality time" is that we should make the most of the little time we have with them.

What exactly does that mean? What do they consider quality time? I love backpacking into rugged wilderness areas and roughing it. My daughter likes riding horses, and my son likes playing video games. Maybe they don't especially like hiking eight miles into the heart of the Eagle Cap Wilderness, living in a little tent, and eating some instant, "just add hot water!" slop. Whose definition of *quality* do we use?

At a pastor's conference a few years ago, our youth department leaders brought in a group of high school students for a panel discussion. We asked this panel of young people, "What constitutes quality time for teens?" They answered, "You parents, forget the idea of 'quality time.' It's a myth. We don't need quality time; we need quantity time. We need you. We need your presence in our lives, whether we're doing some event-packed 'quality' experience or we're just being bored together. We need you, not just some sliver of time you can shave off your busy schedule for us."

Guys, just be with your kids. Let them see you when things are going great and when things don't look so hot. Let them see how you have fun and how you deal with problems. Let them see how much you love their mother, and let them see how you settle family squabbles as a committed partnership.

Since we guys are doers, we're perfectly wired for the role of mentors. A big part of mentoring is doing. I think a good definition of mentoring is, "do something with somebody."

I attended a unique funeral service recently. The young father died in a tragic auto accident. At one point in the service, his wife and kids all came up on the platform to give their personal tributes. What caught my attention was that they were all wearing camouflage gear. This guy involved his family in his love for the outdoors, and this was their way of paying him tribute for spending that time with them. I don't remember what they said in their tributes except for one phrase they each mentioned: "Thank you, Dad, for taking us four-wheeling." This man did nothing that we would think of as exceptional with his life, but what he did made an exceptional difference in the lives of his wife and children. He gave them his time. He mentored his children by sharing what he loved with them, and that will influence them for life.

We have a car for our son to use so he can practice his driving skills. It'll be his when he gets his license. It needed an oil change a while back, and our son needs to know how to change the oil himself, so I thought this was a perfect opportunity to pass on some "guy" family values. Why should he pay a shop $21.95 to change his oil when he can buy the oil and filter, get a little greasy, and save most of that money? But I wasn't exactly sure how to teach him to do it. I determined long ago that I wanted to be an authoritative father. That is a challenge for me, however, because my father practiced the authoritarian model. His parenting style with my siblings and me was more along the lines of exasperating us than patiently mentoring us. He knew only the style of parenting that his dad used in his childhood home. So, I had to consider carefully and consciously, *How would an authoritative father do this?*

I began by asking my son, "Do you want to learn how to change your oil?" To my surprise, he said Yes. So I had him get the tools for me. He didn't know a crescent wrench from a ball-peen hammer, but I described each tool, and he eventually found them and brought them over. I explained each step and why it was necessary. I had him watch me take the drain plug out, and when the oil pan stopped dripping, he replaced the plug. I took off the old filter and he put the new one on. I poured in the first quart of oil, showing him how to do it without spilling it on the engine. (Hint: use a funnel.) He poured in the next three quarts. This whole process took a long time; I could have done it by myself in half the time—but I would have missed a perfect father/son, bonding/mentoring opportunity.

The next time the oil needed changing, I talked him through it. He did all the work, and I didn't touch a wrench or a filter. Now if I keel over dead with a heart attack next time I go hiking, I will die knowing that my son can save some money by doing his own oil changes. Most importantly, though, he got to see how an authoritative parent operates.

Mentoring your kids might eat into your quality time with your guy friends. That's OK. Believe me, your kids' graduations and marriages will come all too soon. Then you can have all the guy time with your friends that you want. Besides that, then you can teach your grandkids all the cool things you do that your kids thought were so corny. Imagine the look on your daughter's face when your granddaughter returns home from a visit with you and sings at the top of her lungs for all the neighbors to hear, "I'm Henry the Eighth I am; Henry the Eighth I am, I am!"

Then it'll all be worth it.

For Personal Reflection

- What spiritual activities do you and your family enjoy together?

- How many of your guy activities do the rest of your family take part in?

- If you could improve one area of your family life, what would it be?

---

* Nancy Darling, "Parenting Style and Its Correlates," *ERIC Digest*, March 1999.

† Ibid.

CHAPTER 12

Did I Say What You Heard?

The title jumped off the magazine cover at me: "Why Don't Guys Talk?" I had to see this.

Sure enough, some woman wrote in to the advice columnist of this magazine with the question, "Why is it that guys never talk?" And the columnist, a female of the species, gave some very deep, well-thought-out counsel. Guys never talk because they fear rejection. Guys never talk because they think they will say something stupid. (Since when has that ever stopped us?) Guys never talk because they get brain-dead nervous around beautiful, intelligent, talented women.

These are all great answers. Unfortunately, they're all wrong. If the columnist were a guy, this is the answer I would have read: "Guys never talk because women never want to talk about four-wheeling, bass fishing, or the playoffs." And isn't the phrase "guys never talk" a little bit of an exaggeration? Of course we talk—to each other! Oh, but I guess we probably should figure out how to talk to non-guys also.

My brother sent me an e-mail recently that has helped me

tremendously in understanding how women communicate. Here are some words that women use and how we should interpret them:

- *Fine.* This is the word women use to end an argument when they feel they are right and you need to be quiet. Never use *fine* to describe how a woman looks—this will cause you to have one of those arguments.
- *Five minutes.* This is half an hour. It is equivalent to the five minutes that your football game is going to last before you take out the trash, so it's an even trade.
- *Nothing.* This means *something,* and you should be on your toes. *Nothing* usually signifies an argument that will last *five minutes* and end with *fine.*
- *Go ahead (with raised eyebrows).* This is a dare—one that will result in a woman getting upset over *nothing* and will end with the word *fine.*
- *Go ahead (normal eyebrows).* This means *I give up* or *Do what you want because I don't care.* You will get a *raised eyebrow–go ahead* in a few minutes, followed by *nothing* and *fine,* and she will talk to you in about *five minutes* when she cools off.
- *Loud sigh.* This is not actually a word, but it is a non-verbal statement often misunderstood by men. A *loud sigh* means she thinks you are an idiot at that moment and wonders why she is wasting her time standing here and arguing with you over *nothing.*
- *Soft sigh.* Again, not a word, but a nonverbal statement. *Soft sighs* mean that she is content. Your best bet is to not move or breathe, and she will stay content.
- *That's OK.* This is one of the most dangerous state-ments that a woman can make to a guy. *That's OK*

means that she wants to think long and hard before paying you back for whatever it is that you've done. *That's OK* is often used with the word *fine* and in conjunction with a *raised eyebrow–go ahead*. At some point in the near future, you're going to be in some mighty big trouble.

- *Please do.* This is not a statement; it is an offer. A woman is giving you the chance to come up with whatever excuse or reason you have for doing whatever it is that you've done. You have a fair chance with the truth, so if you're careful, you shouldn't get a *that's OK*.
- *Thanks.* A woman is thanking you. Don't faint. Just say, "You're welcome."
- *Thanks a lot.* This is much different from *thanks*. A woman will say *thanks a lot* when she is really upset at you. It signifies that you have offended her in some callous way, and it will be followed by a *loud sigh*. Be careful not to ask what is wrong after the *loud sigh*, as she will only say *nothing*.

I hope that helps, because we typically think that what a woman says is what she means. Meaningful communication is often not a guy's strong suit. We can barely speak to each other beyond a few timely grunts, let alone manage effective communication in our homes, so I want to give you some help in that area.

A costly misunderstanding

The communication that preceded the bombing of Hiroshima and Nagasaki provides an excellent illustration of the importance of proper communication.

Every August 6 the same question arises: Did we really need to drop the atomic bomb on these cities? I've heard the same arguments over and over. "We warned the Japanese to surrender or face mass destruction." Yes, but we had said that several times before August 6, so why should they really believe that it would come now? "We needed to drop the bomb to prevent a bloody land invasion." But the bombing raids over Japan had already shattered the Japanese ability to wage war, and they probably would have offered little resistance if we had invaded them.

Historians and ethicists will argue the point until Jesus comes, but the real story may be that the whole episode was the result of a tragic miscommunication. By the spring of 1945, the Japanese leadership knew they'd been soundly defeated. The Allied bombings had destroyed Japan's ability to produce weapons. For months, Japanese planes were being made of cloth stretched over bamboo frames. By September 1945, a lack of aluminum for engine blocks would stop Japanese aircraft production altogether. Allied bombings were destroying roads and railroads faster than they could be rebuilt. Entire cities were leveled. Millions were homeless. The Japanese navy was completely destroyed. Japan's shipping routes were cut off, and the nation was running out of food.

On July 26, 1945, the United States, Britain, and China issued the Potsdam Declaration, demanding unconditional surrender. When the Japanese leaders heard the terms of surrender, they were jubilant. The declaration was much more lenient than they had expected. Emperor Hirohito immediately told his foreign minister, Togo, that the terms of surrender were acceptable. They needed only to confirm it with the full cabinet and then announce it to the world.

Since the news of the Potsdam Declaration had already gotten out to the public, the cabinet needed to say something about their intentions until they could make an official announcement about their surrender. Two days after the Potsdam Declaration was issued, Prime Minister Suzuki told the press that the cabinet was holding to a position of *mokusatsu*. In other words, he said they had "no comment." Now, since Japan's leaders had immediately rejected all other demands for surrender, he expected the Japanese people to understand that this time they hadn't rejected the declaration and would soon negotiate for peace.

However, the word *mokusatsu* has no exact English translation, and it's even tricky for the Japanese to understand. *Moku* means "silence," and *satsu* means "kill." An absolutely literal translation of *mokusatsu* is "to kill with silence." The word actually means either "to withhold comment" or "to ignore."

Suzuki and the Japanese cabinet ministers knew he meant "no comment," but the translators at the news agency didn't know that. They had to choose which meaning would be translated into English and broadcast to the world. The news that Radio Tokyo broadcasted to the world proclaimed that Japan had decided to "ignore" the Potsdam Declaration.

My *World Book Encyclopedia* tells the rest of the story this way: "When Japan ignored the ultimatum, the United States decided to use the atomic bomb."* The two bombs killed 150,000, and wounded another 150,000—all because what one man said was different from what another man heard.

Does that ever happen in your home? (Or shop? Or Sabbath School class?) Are the words you say, the words that your family hears? Are you ever misunderstood? Do you ever misunderstand your wife or co-worker? Have you ever had a major relationship meltdown because of miscommunication? Has your wife ever said, "Well, I knew what I meant"? The problem is that language is tricky. We're all taught how to talk, but very few of us know how to communicate.

If it weren't for the Holy Spirit, we couldn't even pray right. Romans 8:26, 27 says, "The Spirit helps us in our weakness. We do not know what we ought to pray for, but the Spirit himself intercedes for us with groans that words cannot express. And he who searches our hearts knows the mind of the Spirit, because the Spirit intercedes for the saints in accordance with God's will." At least we have the Holy Spirit to intercede and make sure that God understands us. But who interprets our fumbling attempts to communicate with other people?

My one-year-old son invented his own word: *batball.* This word had a variety of meanings, depending on his mood. One day he said, "Throw me batball," so I tossed him his basketball. "No!" he said. "I want batball." So I threw him his softball. "No! No! No! I want batball!" So I tossed him his kickball. "No Dadad, no! I want *batball!*" He wanted his football.

All the different messages

Communication is an intricate process. When we say something, at least six different messages are present:

1. The message that you intend to say. (You compliment your wife on her new dress, and you think, *My wife will love me for saying this!*)
2. The message that you actually say. (You realize, *Oops! That didn't come out exactly as I wanted.*)
3. The message that the other person hears. (She wonders, *Why did he say that?*)
4. The message that the other person thinks she hears. (She's getting indignant: *Is he trying to tell me that I'm fat?*)
5. The message that the other person says. (You, being the wise, intuitive guy that you are, realize that you're in big trouble: *She doesn't love me for saying this!*)
6. The message that you think the other person says. ("Am I even a part of this conversation?")

Sorry, guys. I know we like things plain and simple, but this is the reality of interpersonal communication. It's complicated—but hey, we're guys; we can conquer this too!

But wait, there's more: On top of all the language problems, there is nonverbal communication. You may say one thing, but your clumsy mannerisms can sabotage the whole communication process. In communication, words make up only 7 percent of the message. Vocal intonation is 38 percent, and body language is 55 percent. Charles Spurgeon told his preaching class about the importance of matching your facial expression with your speech. "When you speak of Heaven," he said, "let your face light up; let it be irradiated with a heavenly gleam; let your eyes shine with reflected glory. But when you speak of hell—well, then your ordinary face will do."

Communication is something we take for granted, but in reality it's a bit like walking through a minefield: We need to choose our steps carefully. The Holy Spirit doesn't always translate our messages for us because God gave us counsel in the Scriptures on how to have better communication.

Communication is more than just talking. Proverbs 18:13 says, "He who answers before listening— / that is his folly and shame." Did you ever notice that we spend one year teaching our kids to talk and seventeen years trying to get them to listen? Whether you know it or not, listening begins before a word is ever spoken. We begin by listening with our eyes. We make judgments about people at first sight. A person's clothes, hair, mannerisms, and skin color all influence what we hear with our ears. There are times when you know within the first five seconds after your wife enters the room what kind of interaction you're going to have by her expression and body language. And, especially if it's bad, we immediately begin forming our defense. But when we make sight judgments, we are guilty of answering before listening.

There are other barriers to listening: We stop listening when we start thinking about what our reply will be. We stop listening when we are thinking about some appointment we have to make. (How do you like it when the person to whom you're talking starts looking at his watch?) We stop listening when we don't like what's being said.

A fool answers before he hears all the words. A fool answers before he hears all the ideas, all the feelings, all the joy, all the suffering behind the words. Listening is much more important than talking.

The Bible says that good communication is timely. Proverbs 15:23 says, "A man finds joy in giving an apt reply— / how good is a timely word!" A timely word is said in the right place and the right time.

Here's an example of an untimely word: Let's say you're on your way to take out the garbage without being asked (it could happen!), and you hear your wife in the other room say, "Honey, take out the garbage please." You were doing this out of your own initiative, and now it appears that you had to be nagged to do it. It makes you want to drop the bag of garbage in the middle of the kitchen and tell her "No!"— all because of an untimely word. Don't respond to an untimely word with another untimely word.

This category includes things like forgetting a birthday or anniversary. "How good is a timely word" especially on those particular occasions.

The importance of accuracy

Good communication is accurate. Proverbs 12:18 says, "Reckless words pierce like a sword."

Computer programmers understand this. On July 22, 1962, NASA launched a probe to explore Venus. A computer programmer wrote a command as "DO 3 I = 3.1" instead of "DO 3 I = 3,1." A period instead of a comma sent the rocket blasting toward Miami instead of Venus, and they had to destroy it. Whoever said, "Sticks and stones may break my bones, but words will never harm me," has never been falsely accused of something by a loved one. We must check the accuracy of our words carefully.

Communication must be appropriate. Proverbs 13:3 says, "He who guards his lips guards his life, / but he who speaks rashly will come to ruin." Rash words are often extreme words; words that you wouldn't normally think of saying, except that you are hurt and angry and you want to hurt back. Another proverb says, "A gentle answer turns away wrath" (Proverbs 15:1).

Communication must be simple. First Corinthians 2:1 says, "I didn't use lofty words and brilliant ideas to tell you God's message" (NLT). What are the three simple words your wife longs to hear over and over and over again? "I love you." There are lots of creative ways to say those three simple words, such as Post-it Notes strategically placed in her purse, her coat pockets, or the spaghetti container, with those three words written on them. It may take her months to find some of them, but then it's like you just did it. Flowers, even when you didn't do something stupid that you're trying to make up for. Chocolate. Lot's of it. All the time. Just hand it over, and nobody gets hurt!

Kay Kuzma suggests twelve ways to cherish your wife. These are all practical ways to say, "I love you."

1. Sacrifice something for her.
2. Listen to her.
3. Touch her.
4. Be with her in public.

5. Say kind things about her in public.

6. Share her responsibilities.

7. Let her know you admire her.

8. Show respect.

9. Be an understanding father.

10. Open the doors of possibility for her.

11. Take time to be alone with her.

12. Be the spiritual leader of your family.

These all say, "I love you"—which is the timeliest, most accurate, most appropriate, simplest, and most important message ever communicated.

God heard our pleas for help and communicated His love for us in the life and death of His Son. The life of Christ is God's creative effort to communicate life, hope, and happiness to people who hear only death, despair, and frustration in this world.

For Personal Reflection

- How would you rate the communication in your home: "Never a misunderstanding" or "I can never say anything right"?

- Think about the last big blowup in your home. What was the miscommunication that set it off?

- Identify one thing you can do to be a better communicator.

World Book Encyclopedia (1973).

CHAPTER 13

There's a Time to Laugh

My head elder, Art, and I were discussing a problem at our church school. It was serious stuff—this issue affected teachers, parents, and students alike. And, since our congregation was the only one supporting the school, it could affect the ministry of the whole church. My anxiety level rose with each new revelation about the implications of this problem.

Art, thirty years my senior and much wiser about these things, interjected this into the conversation: "By the way, did I tell you that I ran into Sven and Ole at the lumberyard the other day?"

"No Art, I didn't know that," I replied, wondering where he was going with this. Art, with his Scandinavian background, loved to tell Sven and Ole jokes.

"Yah," he said in his best Norwegian accent. "Sven told the clerk that they needed some four-by-twos.

" 'Four-by-twos?' the clerk asked. 'Don't you mean two-by-fours?'

" 'Yah, two-by-fours,' replied Sven, 'we need some two-by-fours.'

"The clerk asked, 'How long do you need them?'

" 'Oh,' Sven said, 'we'll need them a long time. We're building a house.' "

When I finished groaning at Art's joke, he said something wise that put the church-school problem back into its proper perspective. He had broken the tension with a bit of humor, and we worked through the issue. Now, fifteen years later, the church and school are still operating, and I can't even tell you what the specific details of the problem were. But I remember the joke!

Guys like humor. Unfortunately, most of the humor that guys are exposed to in the workplace and other guy hangouts is inappropriate for a Christian in any setting. The challenge for Seventh-day Adventist guys is to find humor that is both clean and funny. But then, where do you tell these jokes? In Sabbath School? Probably not (and please forget I even suggested that). Sure, there are guy settings that are appropriate for good, clean fun, but sometimes guys feel like there is no room in Christianity for humor. Spirituality may be joyful, but it is also deadly serious. Jesting simply for jesting's sake can be inappropriate.

So what's a guy to do?

Be like Jesus.

Some people have this picture of Jesus as some dour, dismal spoilsport who was always looking for ways to extinguish all the fun in life. Nothing could be further from the truth. Sure, the Scripture says He was a man of sorrows, but then it explains why: He was acquainted with grief. Of course He had His sad times—He was stuck living with *us* for thirty-three years! He knew the joys of living in the cheerful environment of heaven, yet He was exiled to this land of death. I think His preference would have been for all of us to live in the land of endless joy for eternity and never have to deal with the sin mess. He preferred joy and cheer, yet He chose to roll up His sleeves and do the dirty work of salvation to redeem us. I think we can cut Him a little slack when it comes to the serious side of His demeanor.

However, the life and teachings of Jesus contain a humor that we often overlook as we read the Bible through our twenty-first-century, North American glasses. But look deeper and we see One who had a delightful sense of irony and the absurd.

"Isn't it ironic," Christ might say in Matthew 6:16, "that the hypocrites contort their faces to show people how greatly they suffer for the cause, and they hope that others will take notice. Well, it's working! It's plain for all to see how miserable they are. That's their reward. But don't you be dismal like them." This is my paraphrase of Christ's humorous intent in this meaningful lesson. Read it for yourself and see if you get the joke. Now imagine you have been personally chastised by these same hypocrites for not being as dour and dismal as they are. Your Savior just gave you permission to laugh at their absurdity.

How ironic that the wealthy have all the riches and power that this world offers, yet to get to the next life they have to slim everything down to the barest thread, just as a camel would have to go on an extreme crash diet to fit through the eye of a needle (Matthew 19:24). Imagine how empowered oppressed peasants of the first century would feel when they grasped the absurdity of Christ's statement. For the first time they'd realize that they had a better chance at heaven than the most powerful people of the land. That's pure joy!

How ironic that the people who judge the minutest details of your life really can't see a thing about you because they're blinded by the timbers planted on their faces (Matthew 7:3–5). They can't get within twenty feet of you as those planks rotate with their heads and smack into everything around. How absurd that people with such enormous personal problems of their own would even attempt to comment on your microscopic speck of dust. And would you light a candle and put it under your bed (Mark 4:21)? You'd better have good homeowners insurance!

Jesus had a delightful sense of irony and the absurd. And He used it as a powerful communication tool to influence His hearers.

Zingers

Guys often use irony and absurdity and don't know it. They use what are called zingers—one-liners that punch right through to the heart of a matter and make a powerful statement, all in the utterance of a few sharp syllables.

I recently played in a volleyball tournament at a pastors' retreat. I leaped as high as I could to block a ball, but it sailed out of my reach and out of bounds. I made a tongue-in-cheek comment about how I "obviously restrained my jump to let the ball go out." A pastor new to the area called out, "Jump? Is *that* what you call that?" Ouch! That was his way of introducing himself. We're great friends now.

Just like Jesus, guys communicate great truths through humor. What my new pastor friend communicated to me wasn't that I'm a terrible volleyball player, though his comment had a clear ring of truth. His zinger really said, "I like you, and I feel comfortable enough with you to tease you." Somehow, he knew that I would take it as he intended it—with a laugh. I've heard it said that you can tease only people you really like.

A pastor recently moved into a new district, one where I had spent a few years. Joe, a good friend of mine and a guy in every sense of the word, was on the pastoral search committee. The new pastor got a bead on him right away. On the pastor's first Sabbath in his new church, Joe introduced his wife to him. The pastor's first response to this lady was, "You're Joe's wife? You have my condolences!" Joe called me later that afternoon, told me of this exchange, and said, "This guy is all right! I like him!" The pastor knew how to win Joe's trust and friendship guy to guy. Joe is a joker, and the new pastor instinctively knew that the way to Joe's heart is to tease him.

Jesus knew how to tease. When Nathanael first met Him, the Lord proclaimed Nathanael " 'a true Israelite in whom there is nothing false' " (John 1:47). Nathanael may have taken this as a great compliment at first—until Jesus revealed " 'I saw you while you were still under the fig tree before Philip called you.' " Then Nathanael realized that if Jesus had seen him, He also might have heard his comment to Philip, " 'Nazareth! Can anything good come from there?' " Jesus diffused an awkward situation with a little good-natured ribbing.

Jesus christened James and John the "sons of thunder." I can imagine that He cooled their fiery passions many times as He shook His head and simply said, "Looks like the sons of thunder are at it again."

When Jesus met Paul on the road to Damascus, He introduced Himself as the One Paul was fighting against. Then he made the comment, " 'It's hard for you to kick against the goads' " (Acts 26:14). A goad is a sharp-pointed stick used to drive oxen. The oxen might not have liked being driven, but kicking against the goad only added injury to the insult. Jesus' comment was a good-natured way of saying, "You're not going to get anywhere by banging your head against a wall. You're a smart guy. Why don't you quit fighting Me and join Me?" Jesus created a humorous image in Paul's mind to picture the futility of his battle. And Paul got the point. (OK, that's a bad pun. But he never forgot the lesson.)

Dangerous humor

Guys know how to use humor to break the ice in a new relationship (the new pastor and Joe), to release the tension of a stressful situation (Art), and to drive home an important point (Jesus). The danger is that humor can backfire on you. Here are some tips on how to keep your attempts at humor from biting you.

Keep your humor clean. If the topic or the punch line is even a little bit questionable, it's best to just drop it. You risk tarnishing both your reputation and Christ's if someone is even slightly offended by your taste in humor. Besides, you can be the one to show that Seventh-day Adventist guys can enjoy clean fun.

Be keenly aware of potentially touchy people or subjects. The new pastor at the volleyball tournament sensed it was safe to tease me because I was teasing and horsing around with others. Someone else in the tournament, however, took the competition a bit too seriously. When some of us in the stands made humorous comments to try to lighten the mood, we received cold stares in return.

A group of families prepared to go white-water rafting. One couple had never gone before, and both were a bit nervous about it. I started to make a light remark about their concern when the woman said her sister had been killed in a white-water-rafting accident. I nearly swallowed my tongue. My remark, as witty as I'm sure it probably was, would have been terribly offensive. I am so glad she spoke up or I'd still be pulling my foot out of my mouth. Humor can be a sharp, double-edged sword!

Sometimes we guys can get ourselves in trouble because we tend to make smart comments to cover up the fact that we just don't know what to say to make tense situations better. If we can't fix this problem, we feel that we're somewhat less than real men, so we have to deflect people's attention away from our inadequacies. But there are some situations where humor is never appropriate. Generally speaking, for instance, emergency rooms and funeral homes are places where it's best to hold your tongue.

Here are some phrases to try in those situations: "I'm sorry," or "I don't know what to say," or a simple "I love you." And here's some good counsel from Proverbs: "Even a fool is thought wise if he keeps silent, and discerning if he holds his tongue" (17:28). Now that's the true definition of a wise guy!

For Personal Reflection

- Think about the things you used to find funny before you became a Christian. Do those things still seem humorous?

- How did your style of humor change? Did it happen all at once, or was a longer process necessary?

- What would you say to a guy who persists in inflicting inappropriate humor on you? How could you help him change by your personal example?

CHAPTER 14

And a Time to Cry

Art died the other day. He'd been sick for some time, so it wasn't a surprise. Still, it's never easy. He and I had stayed in touch through the years, even though I'd moved three or four times since he was my head elder. I wish I could have fixed the cancer that ate away at his body, but I, like every other guy I know, was helpless.

Art and his wife, Judy, were a team. In fact, they really didn't have individual identities. When we spoke of one of them, we spoke of both. We didn't address them as *Art* or *Judy* but as *Art-'n'-Judy*: "I'm going over to Art-'n'-Judy's," or "I saw Art-'n'-Judy at the store." Their phone number is programmed into my cell phone under the name *Art and Judy*. It seems strange now when someone calls from their home and "Art and Judy" shows up on the caller ID. Now it's just Judy; there is no more Art. I should change the listing on my phone. Maybe I will someday.

I suppose it's a part of the grieving process to want to hang on to something that says this loved one isn't really gone. Or maybe it seems disrespectful to delete someone's name from my phone, as if that person is nothing more than a few pixels on an LCD screen. Or maybe when his name pops up, I remember the guy who could expound such wisdom with a simple Sven-and-Ole joke. I may delete his name from my phone's memory someday, but I hope I never delete his name from my own memory.

How to grieve—that's such a mystery for guys. What works for one may not work for another. Yet, since we are guys, we need a grieving process that *works*. Give us a shop manual, a diagram, a blueprint, a pass play outlined in the dirt that we can run to perfection for a touchdown before our cheering family and friends. But grief isn't something that we can outline and define and pack into a neat little box and put away when we're through with it. It isn't something we can conquer. It isn't a virus that gets us down for a bit until we take the right remedy to kill it and fix our ailing bodies. We can't control it; we can't deny it; and if we don't resolve it in our hearts and minds, it will ruin us in ways that we'd never imagine.

Larry Yeagley, the guru of Adventist grief counselors, says that the majority of interpersonal problems that he's helped people work through can be traced back to an incident of unresolved grief. Grief eats at us from the inside, like the cancer that riddled Art's withered body.

I had no clue how to grieve when my dad died. I was a seventeen-year-old punk with no regard for anyone but myself, and I certainly wasn't going to cry over him. I was tough (I thought), and I could just move on with life (I thought), and nothing could move me or affect me emotionally without my consent (I thought). I barely even made an appearance at Dad's funeral. I sat in the balcony of the church, as far away from the action as I could get. When the casket was opened for people to pay their final respects, instead of going down to join them, I made a quick exit. Within hours I was back to my normal life and routine. Dad was gone—so what?

Eight years later I became a Christian. I thought about Dad from time to time, and I realized I hadn't properly mourned his passing. I wished I had been more mature in my response at the time of his death. But that part of my life was over and done, and you can't turn back the clock. Nothing I could do about it now. Keep moving on.

I moved right into college. I learned plenty about how to help people in their time of loss. I read good books on counseling and working through the grieving process. As the student chaplain at the local Adventist hospital, I got plenty of personal exposure to people in their times of grief and loss. I learned the right words to say at the right times and helped them process their volatile emotions over what was happening to them. I walked them through their anger, their guilt, their disbelief, their confusion, their uncertainty regarding the future—and all the while, I had a time bomb ticking away in my own soul.

The bomb explodes

One Sabbath afternoon I was with a group of friends at the home of one of my college buddies. He was taking a class on small-group evangelism and had invited about a dozen of us over as part of a class project. He used a small-group Bible lesson to guide us through our afternoon session.

The lesson began with an icebreaker to open us up for deeper discussion. It said we were to take a piece of paper and a pencil and draw a circle representing our dinner table when we were thirteen years old. Next we were to draw the chairs around the table and label them with the names of our family members. Then we were to tell our group something significant about each person sitting around our table.

Easy enough. I told about my older brothers and how they tormented me but I loved them anyway. I said that I got to see my baby sister at the hospital when she was born and that I stuck a dart in my other sister's leg one day when we were playing "chicken." I shared how much I admired my mom for volunteering to be a Cub Scout den mother. But when I got to my dad's chair, all I could say about him was, "He's dead." He was dead, and I had tried to bury his memory so I wouldn't have to face my grief over his loss. I had thought his passing meant nothing to me, but boy was I wrong! I started choking up in front of all my friends in this group. *I can't do this*, I thought. *I'm a guy, and we don't do this!*

I'm sure I said something about my dad, but the message the group clearly heard was that his death greatly affected me. The group leader, my college buddy, said something comforting and appropriate, but I didn't want anyone to say something comforting to me. I'm a guy. I shouldn't need comforting. The wall of strength I'd maintained about my dad's death through the years had crumbled like a sandcastle hit by a sneaker wave. I knew then that I needed to resolve my grief over losing my dad. But how? I could help others work through their grief, but they needed my help because they were weak and I was strong. Oh, how hard it is for us guys to let our walls down and be open and vulnerable. I felt like I'd rather let the grief silently corrode my soul than admit that I couldn't handle it.

I began to think about Dad again. I went through all the memories I could dredge up. I put away my own personal feelings about our imperfect relationship and tried to look objectively at his life and why he did some of the things I didn't like. I discovered that I contributed quite a bit to our strained relationship. I don't think I liked the grieving process, the time of reflection; however, it gave me a whole new perspective on Dad.

I learned a bit more about Dad's upbringing. I hadn't known that he was a PK, a preacher's kid, until several years after his death. Now that I am a preacher and have a couple of PKs of my own, I have a deeper understanding of what his childhood was like. I also saw things about his life that I knew but had never before acknowledged. He was a hard worker. Though we were far from rich, barely even middle class, we never felt poor. He was honest. He never drank. He was always home in the evening. He took us camping, hunting, swimming, and fishing. He rarely cussed, and when he did, it was the mildest form. His co-workers loved him. Nobody—I repeat, *nobody*—ever said a bad word about him. He had an honorable reputation with everyone else but me.

I began to miss my dad. I began to mourn not only my dad but also the relationship I could have had with him. I wish he could see me now that I have my life straightened out. I wish he could see his grandchildren and his great-grandchildren. Through this mourning, I've come to the point, twenty years too late, where I can say, "I love you, Dad, and I miss you." But I suppose this is a case of "it's better late than never."

It's been a long process. We guys like to attack problems—to fix them and move on. Maybe if I'd grieved properly thirty-some years ago, the process would have been shorter. But it's still a process that can't be artificially hurried. Somewhere along the way I've cried over losing Dad—more than once, I'm sure. There have been times when I've prayed for forgiveness for not honoring my father as I should have. Jesus forgave me the first time I prayed that prayer, but I guess I still need to face that part of my character from time to time and pray that it never creeps up again. I like to think that I'm more mature now, and that the cancer of unresolved grief over my dad is in remission.

Back to Art

So, Art died the other day. It wasn't a surprise. We knew it was coming. We just hoped that it would be another day, down the road somewhere. Art, always the joker even in his last few days when he was suffering pain, asked his pastor the last time he saw him, "Hey, did you hear that the pope got the bird flu?"

"No, Art," the pastor replied. "I hadn't heard that."

"Yeah," Art whispered. "He got it from one of the cardinals."

We just wished we had a few more days of Art's painful puns.

I went to see Art-'n'-Judy a week before he died. He was ready, and he'd helped his family get ready. He told them, "It's OK to cry—just not too much." In other words, grieving is OK. But work through your grief; heal and move on. It was Art's way of saying that he's OK, he trusts Jesus, and if you do too, everything will be OK.

Art spoke openly about what was coming. He told me, "The doctor says I have a choice. I can take some medicine that will make me miserable and I could live like that for another three months, or I can choose not to take the medicine and have a more pleasant time with my family for three weeks. I think three pleasant weeks with my family sounds better."

Art, being the practical guy he was, told his family not to spend a lot of money on a fancy casket. "Just put me in a pine box and stick me in the ground," he told them. When the family priced the simple pine boxes that were available, Art's son-in-law Cory (a true guy) said, "We can build a better one than this for less." So they went to work.

The guys all gathered in Art's woodshop. They used Art's tools. They tapped into Art's creativity, as in, "How would Dad do this?" And they created a work of art. Literally. Art had his own wood-crafting business on the side, called "Works of Art." So the family gathered to create one more "work of Art" as a tribute to the man they loved.

They built a pine box. They lined the inside with cedar. They bolted saw blades onto the outside of the box and then bolted hammers onto the saw blades with spacers in between. These hammers were the handles for the pallbearers. The women sewed together some upholstery to line the inside of Art's resting place. Then they added the words, "Works of Art" on the outside of the casket with cut-out wooden letters. This family's tribute was truly a work of Art.

But the real work of Art was the process and the people involved in it. The family worked together, as Art had mentored them. They worked with wood, as Art had taught them. And they worked through their grief, as Art had counseled them. While they built the casket, they talked. They talked about the memories—the good, the bad, the funny, and the almost forgotten. They laughed; they cried; they let out the emotions that had built up through Art's long illness. They healed. A family, grieving yet growing, was Art's true legacy. They grieved like real guys.

Someday soon, Art will arise from the grave, and his first words will be, "Who built *this?*" Art's family is resolved to all be there to tell him about the whole process, both the building process and the healing process.

Guys, it's OK to grieve. Be honest about your grief, at least to yourself. When people ask how you are doing, if you don't feel fine inside, don't say, "I'm fine." Say instead, "I'm working through it," or "I have good days and not so good days." You can even say, "This hurts like the devil!" Many guys are afraid that if they're honest, they'll have to really open up and talk and they just don't feel like it. A good, meaningful exchange in these times can go like this:

"How are you doing?"

"I have good days and not so good days."

"I'm so sorry you're going through this."

"Thanks. I appreciate that."

And leave it at that for now. Grief is real. It's universal. It's nothing to be ashamed of. And no one will ever have a better response to one who is grieving than a simple "I'm so sorry." I just read about a guy who even put his arm around another guy's shoulder. The guy's mother had died unexpectedly. He simply said, "I'm sorry," and they just stood there and cried together.

About crying

About crying. I like Art's counsel, "It's OK to cry, just not too much." There is an appropriate amount of crying that helps resolve grief, and it's different for everyone. But here's the real kicker: No one will judge you or look down on you for letting your emotions out. We make it a problem in our own minds, but true friends would never think less of any guy who is wise enough to release the pent-up emotions. Art's pastor and I both got a bit choked up during our portions of his memorial service, and guess what? No one thought any less of us because of it. On the contrary, it helped some others who were stifling their grief to uncork their emotions and begin the healing process. If you want to be the tough guy, then take on the hard task of showing other guys the real way to heal from loss.

Some guys never shed a tear, and yet they deal with loss in other healthy ways. Some come to the point of acceptance of their loss by talking about their memories of their loved ones. Talk about the real person, warts and all. Don't make them perfect saints, and don't savage their reputations. Remember the person as is and acknowledge the mark that he or she has left on your life. Often this looks and sounds like nothing more than just shooting the breeze, but it's actually a healthy way to process the fact that the person is gone and memories are all that's left.

Some guys study their way through their grief. If my car is broken, I can get a shop manual, troubleshoot the problem, and take the appropriate steps to fix it. If your heart is broken because of grief, get a good book on grief recovery and troubleshoot your own issues. Ask your pastor for some good resources, call your local Adventist Book Center or Christian bookstore, or just go to the library. The resources are out there—just get to work on the problem like the real guy that you are!

Create appropriate memorials for your loved one. Art's kids created a "work of Art." Some people put up roadside memorials to those who die in traffic accidents. Why? It's therapeutic and maybe it will remind someone else to slow down or drive sober. Maybe one person's loss can prevent another's. Several men who have lost wives to breast cancer run in our city's annual "Race for a Cure" fundraiser for breast-cancer research. They memorialize their loved ones in a healthy, practical outlet.

Remember to turn to the Lord. Jeremiah, in his grief over the destruction of his city and probably hundreds of his loved ones, wrote these words:

I remember my affliction and my wandering,
    the bitterness and the gall.
I well remember them,
    and my soul is downcast within me.
Yet I call this to mind
    and therefore I have hope:
Because of the Lord's great love we are not consumed,

> for his compassions never fail.
> They are new every morning;
>   great is your faithfulness (Lamentations 3:19–23).

Suffering, loss, and grief never make sense. Only God can bring a sense of hope out of a senseless situation.

Be ready for God to use this experience to make you a minister to someone else. When you experience grief and loss, God "comforts us in all our troubles, so that we can comfort those in any trouble with the comfort we ourselves have received from God" (2 Corinthians 1:4). When you experience the devastating death of a loved one, God is giving you an opportunity to grow in your usefulness for Him. Think of the things you learn from this experience as new tools in your tool belt. If what you do for God and others enhances your spirituality as a guy, here is an area of great need. It may not be what you would choose, but when God calls you to serve Him in this area, the best answer is "Here I am, Lord. Send me."

For Personal Reflection

- OK, you knew this was coming: Do you have any potential time bombs of unresolved grief lurking in your soul? If need be, make a list.

- How do you best resolve grief in your life: By letting your emotions flow, creating memorials, reflecting on memories, or studying your way through the process?

- Can you think of any ways to turn your grief experiences into positive opportunities to help others? What can you do with your grief that will honor God and bless others?

CHAPTER 15

Proof That Guys Are Still Evolving

Jesus said to the guys on the boat, "Come and I will make you fishers of men." And those guys, whose education was limited to catching fish, cleaning fish, cooking fish, mending nets, and rowing the boat, came ashore and began a journey for the ages.

James, Son of Thunder #1, humbly submitted to execution by beheading for the sake of the gospel. John, Son of Thunder #2, wrote what's known as the Gospel of love. Peter, the disciple who usually spoke first and then pulled his foot out of his mouth, later preached a sermon that resulted in the baptism of three thousand people. Tradition has it that he asked to be crucified upside down because he wasn't worthy to die the same death as his Savior.

Matthew was a publican—a tax collector. A tool of Rome. A traitor to the Jewish nation. His job was to collect as much money as he could from his fellow countrymen. Once he gave Rome their cut, the rest was his to keep. Simon was a zealot. He hated Rome and their henchmen, including publicans like Matthew. His sworn duty was to drive out the Romans and take revenge on their puppets. Yet Jesus molded these two into a team that worked together to establish a new religious system that changed not only the world but also the universe for all eternity.

These disciples were all guys whom Jesus transformed from rough thugs who vied for supremacy over each other into humble servants of all. Who says evolution is just a theory? It's just that in Christ's world, it's called *conversion*. And it even happens to guys.

Mark was a rough Alaskan fisherman. Today he's a teacher in a Seventh-day Adventist college.

Steve was a cigarette distributor. He became the head elder in his church.

John was a bar bouncer. He now pastors three churches.

Joe left his faith but returned to organize a team of lay people to preach a powerful evangelistic series in his church.

Clark was once "too tough to need Jesus," but he became the personal ministries leader in his church.

Curt was a longhaired partier who appeared at my church halfway through an evangelistic series. He later established a television ministry in our church that is still influencing the community over a decade later (and he never cut his hair as long as I was the pastor there).

Ken was a drunken, party-hearty railroad grunt who led me to Christ and the three angels' messages.

And I was, well, someone that you wouldn't want to have as your neighbor (judging by my former neighbors, who used to call the cops on me regularly). Now I'm the guy writing these words that I'm hoping are blessing your soul.

Guys can be transformed by the love of Jesus and the power of His Holy Spirit. They can love Jesus and still be guys at heart. And God can do powerful things through guys who are fully committed to Him.

Who are you at heart? If you don't know the answer to that question, I'll tell you: You're a sinner. Don't take offense to that. I'm a sinner at heart too. So were Peter, and Paul, and Moses, and John, and every person who's ever lived except Jesus. The good news is that Jesus believes in evolution—the evolution from a sinner to a saint. This happens through a process that guys can embrace. It's simple, it's a formula, it's easy to remember, and it works. That's perfect for any guy. It's as easy as ABC:

- "*All* have sinned and fall short of the glory of God" (Romans 3:23; emphasis added). So what if you're a sinner—so is everyone else. If you recognize that you have some things in your life that are out of whack—good! You have a firm grasp of reality. If you can't see anything in your life that needs repair, you have bigger problems than you even imagine. If you need some clues on some areas of improvement that you need to address, go ask your wife/girl-friend/mother. You have to begin at the beginning, the letter A. All have sinned, and that includes you.

- " '*Behold!* the Lamb of God who takes away the sin of the world!' " (John 1:29, NKJV; emphasis added). A famous preacher once said, "I only know two things. Number one—there is a God. Number two—I'm not Him." As a guy, you can fix your car, you can fix your house, and you can even fix broken relationships when you put your mind to it, except one. You can't fix the rift that your sin has caused between you and God. You're not that skilled a repairman. Only Jesus can mend this ruptured relationship. So, A—you have a problem. B—Jesus is the solution to your problem. How do you apply the solution to your problem?

- " '*Come* to Me, all you who labor, . . . and I will give you rest' " (Matthew 11:28, NKJV; emphasis added). Jesus is opening the door of His shop to you right now. Come in and let Him go to work on your broken life. That's the hardest thing for some guys. We can change our own oil, so why should we go to some fancy shop and have it done? But when it comes to our spiritual "oil," we should, because when Jesus changes it, He replaces the worn-out old oil with the oil of the Holy Spirit. It never wears out. It is always fresh and clean and new. And you can't get it anywhere else. Once you've had your oil changed by Jesus, once you've experienced true conversion, you'll never want to try to do it yourself again.

What's the price of this heavenly oil change? Nothing, to you. As a great old hymn puts it, "In my hand no price I bring; / simply to Thy cross I cling." A new life for eternity is there for you to claim. All of heaven is standing on the sidelines, cheering you on, watching with breathless anticipation for you to reach out and claim your prize.

It's as simple as ABC. You can evolve from a sinner to a saint. You can be a new person—still a guy, but a converted, sanctified, Spirit-filled guy. I believe that heaven needs more guys. I know that heaven needs you.

For Personal Reflection

- In what areas of your life do you obviously fall short of the glory of God? Identify them, but don't beat yourself up over them. You are no better or worse than anybody else.

- When you behold the Lamb of God who takes away the sin of the world, what do you see—Someone who could never love a sinner like you or Someone who gave His life to save you?

- Have you accepted Christ's invitation to come? If so, reflect on the peace and satisfaction you've received. If not, why not? What is keeping you from taking that step?

A Parting Shot

Well, my days as the lone hobo of Hobo Camp are ending. Good thing I've been here this long, because the rainy weather has finally cleared up enough to allow the musty old canvas to dry so I can fold up this tent trailer and tow it home. I can return to civilization and go back to being a regular dad, son, brother, husband, pastor, and friend. But I'll always approach these relationships as a regular guy.

I hope you've had a chance to explore what it means to be a Seventh-day Adventist guy. I hope you know that you have permission to be who God created you to be. I hope you can use the unique identity that God has imprinted in your heart for His honor and glory. And most of all, I hope to meet you in heaven someday soon. I can't wait to swap stories with you. I'm sure that there is some sort of heavenly videotape system so I can show you the footage of the time I almost rolled my Land Cruiser down the mountain. We'll even get to see the angel put out his hand to steady it as it teetered over the edge. I want you to think about the events and miracles that you want to show me. Hey, we'll need some way to pass the time for the next hundred gazillion years!

Before I quit writing, I want to leave you with some helpful advice. Sometimes it seems as though the women establish all the rules of the house. Well, it's time for us guys to reclaim our rightful place as head of the home. I challenge you to establish and enforce the following rules, which a pastor friend sent me a while back. These rules can transform your home and your family relationships. Call a family counsel to introduce them. Post them on your fridge and on the mirrors in your bathrooms and your dressers. Take a stand and see how it transforms your home life.

The Rules From the Male Side

- Ask for what you want. Let's be clear on this one: Subtle hints do not work! Strong hints do not work! Obvious hints do not work! Just say it!
- Yes and No are perfectly acceptable answers to almost every question.
- Crying is blackmail.
- Come to us with a problem only if you want help solving it. That's what we do. Sympathy is what your girlfriends are for.
- Anything we said six months ago is inadmissible in an argument. In fact, all comments are null and void after seven days.
- If something we said can be interpreted two ways and one of those ways makes you sad or angry, we meant the other one.
- Christopher Columbus did not need directions, and neither do we.
- All men see in only sixteen colors (red, green, blue, yellow, orange, brown, black, white, etc.). Peach, for example, is a fruit, not a color. Pumpkin is also a fruit. We have no idea what mauve is, nor do we care.

- If we ask what is wrong and you say "nothing," we will act as if nothing is wrong. We know you are fibbing, but it's just not worth the hassle.
- If you ask a question you don't want an answer to, expect an answer you don't want to hear.
- When we have to go somewhere, absolutely anything you wear is fine. Really.
- Don't ask us what we're thinking about unless you are prepared to discuss such topics as baseball, the shotgun formation, or monster trucks.
- You have enough clothes.
- You have too many shoes.
- Food is as exciting for us as handbags are for you.
- I am in shape. Round is a shape.
- Thank you for reading these rules. Yes, I know I have to sleep on the couch tonight. I don't mind; it's like camping.

OK, I presented these rules to my wife, and she's still doubled up on the floor laughing. The truth is that none of our family rules actually changed, but at least my list was good for a chuckle. Let me know if any of you actually post these rules and apply them in your home. You could be the subject of a new book!

God has made you for a reason, and He's matched you up with your family and friends for a reason. Keep exploring the purpose of your life and then give it all to God. May God bless you as you continue to grow in your understanding of who you are in His eyes.

Hey Guys! Here are some more books you'll like!

Discovering God's Will
Troy Fitzgerald

Does God play hide-and-seek with His will?

Does finding God's will for your life seem like a game show in which you must choose door A, door B, or door C? Can you choose the right door without knowing what is behind it?

Troy Fitzgerald, Ph.D., shares his conviction that you *can* know God's will and live happily in it. In Part 1: The Search for God's Will, you will find answers to your questions and learn principles of guidance. Part 2: The Discovery of God's Will points you to Scripture passages that will help you discover and do God's will, choose God's will over your own, and accept God's will even in times of adversity. Part 3: The Will to Live—Doing God's Will shows you how to distinguish between devotions and devotion in living God's will each day. Learn how God's will can help you make other major life decisions such as choosing a career or finding a spouse.

Paperback, 144 pages.   US$12.99.
ISBN 13: 978-0-8163-2180-3   ISBN 10: 0-8163-2180-9

Cleansing Fire, Healing Streams
Kent A. Hansen

Kent A. Hansen is one of those who has looked thoughtfully, considered his own condition, and been changed by God's grace. "I write my personal experience not to bare my soul, for that alone helps no one," he says. "I am telling you out of my personal knowledge about the cleansing and healing that is possible with Jesus Christ."

The brief and honest chapters in this book will appeal to men and women. Read them in silence and solitude. Let the underbrush and overgrowth of busyness burn away. Make way for the cleansing springs of grace to flow again through your heart and soul, and share what you discover with others.

Paperback, 288 pages.   US$16.99
ISBN 13: 978-0-8163-2179-7   ISBN 10: 0-8163-2179-5

Order from your ABC by calling **1-800-765-6955**, or get online and shop our virtual store at **http://www.AdventistBookCenter.com**.
- Read a chapter from your favorite book
- Order online
- Sign up for e-mail notices on new products

Prices subject to change without notice.